Ava's Story

Miracles Happen

JENNIFER ROHDE DICKERSON

May Peace be with you.

♥ Jennifer

WESTBOW
PRESS
A DIVISION OF THOMAS NELSON

WestBow Press books may be ordered through booksellers or by contacting:

WestBow Press
A Division of Thomas Nelson
1663 Liberty Drive
Bloomington, IN 47403
www.westbowpress.com
1-(866) 928-1240

Because of the dynamic nature of the Internet, any web addresses or links contained in this book may have changed since publication and may no longer be valid. The views expressed in this work are solely those of the author and do not necessarily reflect the views of the publisher, and the publisher hereby disclaims any responsibility for them.

Any people depicted in stock imagery provided by Thinkstock are models, and such images are being used for illustrative purposes only.

Certain stock imagery © Thinkstock.

ISBN: 978-1-4497-4971-2 (hc)
ISBN: 978-1-4497-4972-9 (sc)
ISBN: 978-1-4497-4973-6 (e)

Library of Congress Control Number: 2012907885

Printed in the United States of America

WestBow Press rev. date: 05/18/2012

Contents

Illustrations

To Hope

So teach us to count our days
that we might gain a wise heart.

Psalm 90:12

Acknowledgments

To Nancy Sisler, RN: Thank you for teaching me how to be a mom in the NICU. I always looked forward to Sundays and Mondays. I will never forget the love and care you gave Ava like she was your own daughter. And I will never forget that Tuesday you came in to take care of her.

To Dr. Li Ern Chen: Thank you for caring for Ava even before she was born. Your compassion combined with your expertise is a gift and testimony to the medical profession. There are few words that can express the immense respect I have for you as a person and as a surgeon. I am honored to call you my friend.

To Dr. James Thomas: You comforted us in times of worry and assured us in times filled with unknowns and challenges. You treated my family, not just Ava. The professional care from your expertise and from your heart went above every expectation that any parents could hope for for their child. We will always be grateful for you and your team at Children's. Your kind words about Ava will forever be etched in my heart.

To Dr. Kathy Kordy and Dr. Carrie Herbert: The care you gave Ava went over and above all expectations of the exceptional doctors you are. Thank you for being there with us every day, even on your occasional day off.

To Ralph, RT: Your kind spirit, warm heart, and big smile always brightened our days and filled them with hope. Thank you for taking such great care of our little girl and the machine that supported her life.

To Ester, RT: Our nights with you were always encouraging. Thank you for keeping Todd company while he shared the night shifts with you. Your love for children shows through your work.

To all of Ava's doctors, nurses, respiratory therapists, and ECMO specialists: There are too many to personally name, but please know that you all made a difference in Ava's life and in mine. Thank you all from the bottom of my heart for caring for our little angel.

Dr. Julie Lo: Thank you for giving me those first few seconds with Ava. They are now precious memories I hold very close in my heart.

To my Alpha Phi sisters: Like the ivy that twines, your continued love and support are what binds us together. Your acts of kindness brightened my darkest days. AOE

To Nancy, Erika, and Miriam: Thank you for holding our company together and allowing me to be with Ava and my family without worry. Thanks for hanging on and helping through this past year.

To Dr. Thomas Stieglitz: Thank you for your support from Chicago. Our conversations reassured and clarified my effort to learn and understand the medical world.

To my extended family: You all were the glue that kept us together. I would not have been able to stay by Ava's side day and night without all of your emotional and physical support. I am so blessed to be a part of our wonderful family.

To Mom and Dad: I am grateful for the qualities I possess as a parent because of you. Your love and support throughout my entire life has made me the person I am today. Thank you for always being here for me.

To Todd: My husband, my love, my everything.

Introduction

On September 30, 2010, at thirty-six weeks pregnant, Todd and I were at a weekly prenatal checkup with my obstetrician (OB), Dr. McKown. I had lost a few pounds, and Ava had not grown from the prior week's checkup. Dr. McKown thought a sonogram would be best, just so we could chart that everything was progressing along normally. I took Todd home, finished up work, and was back for the afternoon sonogram appointment. I had not had an official sonogram for a few months, so I was anxious to see Ava on screen again!

After thirty minutes of the ultrasound technician looking and not saying anything, my heart grew heavy. She left the room and then came back to look again. I asked her what she saw, and she told me she just took the pictures and the doctor read them. Tears started streaming down my cheeks. She left, and Dr. McKown's colleague came in. I sat up, and Dr. Patton started to tell me Ava's heart was on the wrong side of her chest and her stomach was very small. I was to go directly across the street and check into labor and delivery for another test. I made it to the car and called Todd. When I told him what was happening, I felt my world beginning to turn upside down.

Todd and I checked into L&D at Methodist Central Hospital in Dallas. Dr. Patton met us and did another sonogram. She set up an appointment for the next morning, Friday, with a maternal fetal medicine specialist (MFM), with whom we had had first- and second-trimester screenings a few months before. We were cleared to go home for the evening, but Dr. Patton said that depending on the next day's appointment, I might have to be induced. We went home, packed our bags, and tried to make sense of the day.

Todd, my mom, and I arrived for our appointment on Friday hopeful that the detailed sonogram would show that Ava was ready to make her debut into our world. Instead, the doctor said Ava more than likely had a condition called congenital diaphragmatic hernia (CDH). After explaining the little he knew about CDH, I asked about survival rates in babies with this condition. He said the mortality rate is 55 percent. My heart shattered; I could barely breathe. He suggested we get a fetal MRI and set up an appointment with Dr. Twickler at University of Texas Southwestern Medical Center (UT Southwestern) the following Monday morning. We walked out into the waiting area in silence and sat down. No one said anything as we tried to comprehend and remember those big words that had been thrown at us: *congenital diaphragmatic hernia*. After a while, the receptionist came over and asked if we needed anything. *Where do we go from here? What am I supposed to do now? I packed my "go bag" last night, and Howard came over to put the pack and play together. Todd . . . Mom . . . what's happening?*

I do not remember much after the appointment except Todd driving to my parents' house, where we ended up staying for the rest of the weekend. That night, I frantically searched the Internet with a box of Kleenex. I was upset that this specialist, with whom we had had early screenings, had not detected this condition before. I learned that CDH is usually found between fourteen and twenty weeks. He had done three sonograms on Ava in that timeframe! How could something be wrong when I'd had a healthy pregnancy? I tried to stay positive, but with statistics that half of the babies do not survive, all I could wonder was how I would go into her nursery full of clothes, diapers, stuffed animals, rattles, and blankets without her. I finally went back to bed to find Todd awake. We cried together as I told him everything I had just learned about CDH.

CDH occurs in approximately one in every 2,500 births, with 1,600 cases in the United States each year. The cause of CDH is not yet known. The diaphragm is formed in the first trimester of pregnancy and controls the lungs' ability to inhale and exhale. CDH occurs when the diaphragm fails to form or to close totally and an opening allows abdominal organs into the chest cavity, thus inhibiting lung growth.

Every patient diagnosed with CDH is different. Survival rates depend on the types and number of organs involved in the herniation and the amount of lung tissue available. There are many surgical procedures and complications that may or may not occur with each individual, including in utero surgery.

Roughly 50 percent of babies born with CDH do not survive. Of the 50 percent that do survive, most will endure long hospital stays, feeding issues, asthma, and other problems. A few of the survivors suffer from severe, long-term medical issues.

The next day, I sat outside with my parents, and we realized that Dr. McKown had saved Ava's life. If she had not ordered that sonogram, Ava's CDH would have gone undiagnosed and she would have been born at the wrong hospital with unprepared doctors. We decided then to find the best doctors for Ava and become as prepared as possible to welcome our miracle baby into this world.

I kept an online journal to keep family and friends updated on Ava's progress. Ava continues to touch lives today. She taught me more about love, faith, and hope than I had ever known, without her ever speaking a word. The following chapters are her story taken from that online journal. Chapter 1 begins with Ava's fetal MRI with Dr. Twickler, who is world-renowned in her field. This appointment was our first step in Ava's CDH journey.

CHAPTER 1

Finding Hope

My mom, Todd, and I checked in for Ava's MRI. When it was finished, we met in Dr. Twickler's office, where she explained her findings and confirmed that Ava did indeed have a left-sided CDH. We immediately connected with her, as she showed compassion and care for Ava while explaining this condition on which she had done extensive research.

Dr. Twickler said I had just gone from a completely normal pregnancy to the highest-risk pregnancy. Ava was safe for the moment, but the complications would start after birth when the umbilical cord was cut. Dr. Twickler told us that she had seen four CDH babies in that past year, but I was too scared to ask how those babies were doing now.

After we decided we wanted to be at the UT Southwestern System, which includes Parkland Hospital and Children's Medical Center of Dallas, for Ava's delivery, surgery, and recovery, we were put on the fast track to assemble a team of doctors for Ava's care. That afternoon, we had an echocardiogram of Ava's heart with a cardiologist from Children's. Nancy, a fetal coordinator from Children's, called the next day to tell me about a family meeting with doctors, surgeons, and nurses to evaluate Ava's condition. We would meet this team one week from today.

We knew we had found the right place for Ava to begin her life. The staff at the UT Southwestern system was exceeding all our expectations. Every day we were learning more about CDH and accepting the challenges that lay ahead. Nancy put us in touch with a family, the Studdards, who had given birth to twin girls in 2009 at Parkland. One of their girls, Kamryn, was diagnosed with CDH at a thirteen-week sonogram. I contacted her mom, Stephanie, and they invited us to their home for dinner.

Two days later, we met with an MFM, Dr. Zaretsky, who had delivered the Studdard twins. He did an assessment of Ava's condition in respect to lung-to-head ratios and of how much liver was herniated, and analyzed another sonogram. "She's got a real good chance," he said with a smile, giving us hope. It was the first time I started to feel better about giving birth to Ava. For the past several days, I had been so scared that I would go into labor and we would not be prepared. He referred me to his colleague, Dr. Julie Lo, to be my new MFM/OB and to deliver Ava. My mom, Todd, and I left with a good feeling for Ava.

The following week, Todd and I met with Dr. Lo. She showed such compassion and care for Ava and for us that we immediately connected with her, and I learned I would still get to experience a regular labor and delivery. She explained she would set Ava on my tummy as she cleaned her off and that Todd would get to cut her cord. I would get to have skin-to-skin contact with my baby Ava for a few seconds! We set the induction date for October 22, 2010. Just ten more days, and we would get to meet Ava Elaine!

That evening, we had dinner at the Studdards' home. We had read their blog that charted Kamryn's daily progress. Shawn, Kamryn's father, wrote "A Parents' Guide to CDH," which really helped Todd and me understand what we were about to experience and what Ava's daily challenges would be right after birth to weeks after.

I was touched that complete strangers invited us to dinner so they could help prepare us for what lay ahead. Oh, their babies were adorable! Kamryn had stayed in the neonatal intensive care unit (NICU) for forty-eight days and came home on her mom's birthday. Shawn showed us her scar from the hernia repair surgery, which was the only thing different from her twin, Brooke.

The girls were just getting tucked in, and I was so happy to meet them and their eight-year-old sister, Hollie. Shawn and Stephanie shared emotional stories about their experience, and we so appreciate their reaching out to us.

Two things I will carry with me through this journey: Shawn and Stephanie told us, "Never lose hope, but don't let it cloud the reality of the situation" and "We can prepare your heads, but no one can prepare your hearts."

Guestbook entries:

Jennifer and Todd,

You both know that you and Ava are constantly in our prayers and have occupied our thoughts for the last week. We are here for anything you might need and able to come help out with anything you might need down there (Jason, Maggie, Jack, the girls, your dogs, etc.). Just let us know of anything we can do! We are praying specifically for Ava's little lungs that the Lord will breathe a big breath of air in them as soon as she is born. We are also praising God that she has wonderful doctors and nurses to help her grow! She is going to be an amazing little girl, and she is so lucky to have such amazing loving parents! You are surrounded by a family that loves you all so much, and we can't wait to share that love with our newest addition to the family!

Love to all,
Aunt Bec

~

Our prayers and thoughts are with you and Todd.

I've sent this on to all the prayer warriors I know, and we *will* be vigilantly praying.

Jennifer, if there is *anything* I can do, please don't hesitate to call or ask.

I will be there in a heartbeat for you and Todd.

Always,
Jennifer

~

Jennifer,

I've read this e-mail over and over since first receiving it early this morning. I've wondered what I should say to you or what I would want to hear if I were you. This is what I have come up with.

Every thought and prayer I have is coming your way. I can guarantee you that from my whole family. If there is *anything* I can do for you, please do not hesitate to let me know. Please put me on a list to be called or e-mailed once Ava is born. I have so much faith about this: she is going to be *fine*, and you will laugh with her one day about all the drama her debut created.

Please know I am *constantly* thinking of you.

Love, Daphne

CHAPTER 2

———— ⌘ ————

Family Meeting with Ava's Doctors, Surgeons, and Nurses

My mom, Todd, and I were in the center of the room with twenty-five people who had studied Ava's case and were preparing for her birth. After introductions, the lead doctor detailed what would happen as soon as Ava was delivered to the hours and days after.

There were two scenarios which he referred to as Book A and Book B. These were not the books that you could jump to the back of and see the ending. Ava would decide her story hour by hour, day by day, and week by week.

Book A had so many different possibilities. Major issues, risks, and complications associated with those possibilities were explained to us. A high-risk team of resuscitation nurses would be on standby. After my moment of skin to skin, Ava would immediately be put on a ventilator during her first breaths of life outside my tummy. Her heart and lungs would be analyzed in her first few hours. The doctor explained that her repair surgery would be performed as soon as possible, once she was stable enough to endure surgery. Her liver, spleen, intestines, and other organs would be pulled back down into her stomach cavity, allowing her lungs and heart the room they needed to grow. Some CDH babies with extreme lung damage must be put on a life support machine called extracorporeal membrane oxygenation (ECMO). ECMO is a heart and lung bypass machine that lets those organs rest and recover. During the past week I had researched as much as possible about CDH. I read a lot about ECMO and how it had saved many lives of CDH babies. Children's was equipped with at least five ECMO machines, just in case Ava needed one. *Just in case.*

Book B had many possibilities, too, but was not so much in Ava's control. Things like comfort care and knowing when to let go were part of this book. As I passed the box of Kleenex to my mom, I thought Ava and I were going to be talking a lot in the next few weeks about reading Book A.

As our meeting was adjourned, a sweet, young lady introduced herself to us as Dr. Chen. She would be the surgeon on call the weekend I was to be induced and would perform Ava's repair surgery. I thought it was nice of her to go out of her way to let us know Ava would be in good hands during surgery.

We left feeling informed, prepared, and scared at the same time. We were ready, though, and anxious to meet our little girl.

CHAPTER 3

Happy Birthday, Ava

Ava Elaine Dickerson was born October 22, 2010 at 11:32 p.m., weighing six pounds and six ounces. I know all the parents out there know that childbirth is an amazing gift from God. I did get skin-to-skin contact for a few seconds while Todd cut her cord. I will never forget those precious moments. They took her immediately to the station in the room, and she was surrounded by the resuscitation team who stabilized her lungs. Before she left, they brought her to me so I could give her a good-bye kiss.

Todd and my mom were in the NICU with Ava while she was getting an echo on her heart. My mom came back and said she was a fighter and had tight fists as they were working on her. We were praying for Ava and her doctors and nurses, as the next few days were so critical.

By midnight I was anxious and ready to be wheeled into the Parkland NICU to see Ava. She was absolutely beautiful. I did not care about the tubes, wires and monitors; all I wanted to do was put my hand on her tiny head full of red hair (*Where did that come from?*) and tell her everything was going to be just fine. *Don't be scared, Mommy is right here.*

Guestbook entries:

Dear Jennifer,

She is beautiful! Thank you for sharing the picture. Grandma sends her love—I have been forwarding your e-mails to her. She told me she just kept reading them over and over and thinking about that little girl. At her church service in the nursing home, they ask if anyone wishes to make a prayer request, and she gave Ava's name and told her story. So she has two hundred octogenarians praying for her. Stay strong.

Much love,
Aunt Debby

~

Praying, praying, praying . . .

I wouldn't expect anything less than a fighter, knowing how strong her mother is.

She is absolutely beautiful . . .

I am so glad you got a few moments of skin to skin and were able to kiss her.

Not even for a second have I ever grown tired of kissing my boys.

I am praying, celebrating, and praying some more for you and your new family.

We love you more than words can express, and can't wait to meet your precious gift from God.

I've always said, "How can anyone who's had a baby deny there is a higher power than ourselves?!"

All our love,
The Baileys

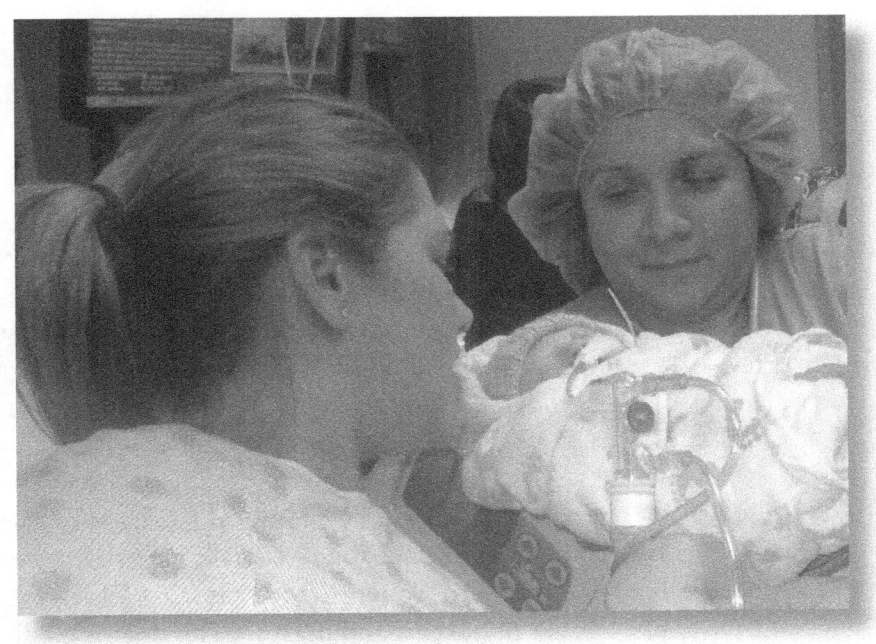

The Journey Begins

**The nurses bring Ava for a kiss before leaving
for the NICU.**

CHAPTER 4

———⚬⚬⚬———

Minute to Minute

Ava has gone through more in the first two days of her life than I could ever imagine. The nurses and doctors told us all of these things could happen but to see our sweet baby Ava struggle and fight for her life is really hard. She has had great hours and not so great hours. Last night a few of her levels got critical enough for her team of doctors at Parkland to recommend a transfer to Children's intensive care unit (ICU). Children's has ECMO machines, and they felt it was best to transfer her while she was still strong enough in case she needed to be put on ECMO. A team from Care Flight assembled the transfer cart equipped with oxygen and monitors. Todd was talking to a doctor about the details of the transfer: "When she makes it to Children's, will we have a different set of doctors and nurses?" The doctor coldly replied, "If she makes it, you will have a new . . ." Todd interrupted with a loud "*If she makes it?*" The doctor said the transfer was very risky but had to be done in order to give her a chance to survive. As they started to wheel the transfer cart down the hallway to Children's, monitors started beeping all at once and the doctors stopped, as did all of our hearts. They stabilized Ava, and we started again, step by step, and got her to Children's NICU. A respiratory therapist did a suction procedure through her vent tube and took out a few mucus plugs that were blocking her tiny airways. Ava settled down in her new room with improved numbers. They stayed stable and even improved throughout the day.

Around 7:45 p.m. she started to decline again, and I felt like she told us she needed a little break. The team recommended that they perform the surgery to put her on ECMO. This machine takes the blood out of her body, oxygenates it, and then pumps it back to her so her lungs may rest. Dr. Chen, was on call. She greeted us and I felt my nerves calm knowing she was in great hands. We had two surgeons (Dr. Chen and Dr. Megison) along with her nurses and the ECMO team, all regarded as the best, operate on our little girl. (*Now that I reflect back on this journal entry, I remember the most important thing of that night. I have mixed feelings about how rushed we were, but nonetheless, it will go down as one of Ava's most significant days of her life.*)

As the doctors and nurses transformed her room into an operating area, we tried to understand the depth of what was happening. Dr. Chen had just presented a form for Todd and me to sign. My heart was breaking as she had to explain the risks and potential complications of this surgery that had to be performed to save Ava's life. The last risk was death. I had to sign something saying I acknowledged Ava may die during this procedure. I remember Todd literally having to hold me up. We signed the form and then a chaplain appeared with open arms and kind words. We all held hands and prayed for Ava and her team. My mom, Todd, and I were allowed back by her bed as our sweet baby Ava was baptized.

My dad and Aunt Becky came to the hospital. All five of us sat in a family room and waited. The two strongest men I knew were right next to me and looked worried and scared. The doctors had told us this could happen. *She's only two days old. Please God, please let Ava make it through this surgery.*

Dr. Chen delivered the news that the surgery went well and Ava was stable and resting. We all exhaled at the same time as I reached out to hug Dr. Chen.

Ava's numbers look good and her lungs will be able to rest and recover while on ECMO. It's now hour to hour and Team Ava is still strong, hopeful, and faithful.

I believe all of your love, prayers, and support for Team Ava has given her the strength to be a fighter and survivor. She opened her beautiful eyes today while Todd and I were by her bed. She told me with her eyes she will make it through this fight. Another precious moment I will cherish forever. Please continue to keep us in your thoughts and prayers . . . we appreciate everyone so much!

Guestbook entries:

Jen and Todd, thank you for the update. Aunt Bec has been keeping us well informed. I went to Aunt Barb's today and saw the picture of Ava right after birth. She is adorable! You have quite a little girl there. She might be small, but she's mighty. (She has that good Rogy stock, don't ya know?] I know it's hard seeing your little girl go through this, and you will remember this for the rest of your lives, and she won't have a clue what you all were so worried about. Keep in mind this machine is saving her life, and along with Ava's determination not to miss the big party planned for her, and along with one of the best mommies in the world, she would be the first one to say if she could, "I'm not missing this life for no one!" I love you all so much and will be seeing you soon.

Love, Aunt Lori

~

Thank you for sharing with us Jennifer. Ava, you, and Todd are in my prayers. There is absolutely *nothing* impossible to *God*, and I know *He* will be by your side through this.

Love,
Erika

CHAPTER 5

———∽∾∼———

Repair Surgery Scheduled

Todd and I had lengthy discussions today with Ava's lead surgeon, Dr. Chen, about the details of her hernia repair. She is strong enough for surgery now, which allows her to stay on ECMO postsurgical to recover. She will have an incision on her lower left abdomen, and they will pull her liver, bowels, stomach, and spleen back down under her diaphragm. If the hole is too big to repair with just the muscle, they will stitch a patch made of an organic material called Permacol to complete her diaphragm. Permacol will allow scar tissue to form and grow with Ava. Her room will be converted into the operating room, and the surgery should take about two hours.

Ava is responding remarkably well to ECMO. Her lungs and heart are getting needed rest as this ECMO machine, which has a specialist sitting next to it twenty-four hours a day, works to keep her safe. She was responding to us today by lifting her arm, wiggling her feet (so cute!), and opening her eyes to look around. I think these are all signs from Ava letting us know she's ready for surgery.

She got a new machine last night that helps the kidney to function, because her fluid output decreased (normal for ECMO). This machine was integrated with the ECMO machine and helps her with the fluid output (she's going potty more now). This morning, the night nurses told Todd she's producing by herself, which is great, but they will keep the machine for precautionary measures.

At rounds this morning, the doctors were very pleased with the last twenty-four hours. The head of pediatric intensive care unit (PICU), Dr. Thomas, has consulted with the surgeons and scheduled

Ava's surgery for 10:00 a.m. tomorrow. We find it encouraging that they are talking about an early repair surgery while on ECMO.

Highlights from the last twenty-four hours: Ava got her first sponge bath, the nurses let my mom and me put lotion on her, she squeezed her daddy's hand, the nurses taught me how to take her hourly body temperature, and most importantly, her numbers are right on target and steady. She's our little superstar.

I realized last night, even though being at Children's means Ava is in a more critical condition, there are many benefits, especially for Ava. She's got a private room that's quiet and calm. Todd and I can stay with her twenty-four hours a day (and my mom too, since they are letting us bend the rules). The doctors and nurses want us involved with every step of her care. They encourage us to be present and ask questions during their daily rounds.

We are so moved by the amount of love and support we've received over the past few weeks. We have otherwise strangers calling, visiting us at the hospital, and e-mailing us to show their support for Ava. All of your prayers, love, and support for Ava will get her through surgery and recovery. Thanks to each one of you; we truly appreciate you reaching out and spreading the love for Ava.

CHAPTER 6

———⚬⚬⚬———

The Roller Coaster

Let me introduce you to the roller coaster we are on. About forty-five minutes before surgery, Ava's little legs started losing color. They were cold and the pulses in her feet were very weak. An emergency chest x-ray showed a blood clot in her abdomen. This is an immediate threat and has to be fixed before surgery is performed. They are in the process of administrating a drug to break up the clot which will delay the surgery for at least twenty-four hours. The good news is she's stable and will be able to rest until the doctors clear her for surgery.

God is watching over her. If this had happened during surgery, it would have added risk and complications.

Guestbook entries:

> Parenthood *is* a roller coaster ride—however, for most of us, the ride is not nearly as scary, dramatic, or life-threatening as the one you and Todd are currently taking. To my way of thinking, another sign that God is watching over Ava is that she has you and Todd for parents. Hang in there.
>
> Duke

~

15

Jennifer and Todd,

My good friend Elaine has asked several people to pray for Ava. Below is a response she received from a relative of hers.

Danny and I just had prayer for her again. It was hard to get the words out because of my tears, but I know God knows my heart and the Holy Spirit cleaned it up as he presented it to our awesome God. I also prayed late last night. Please let me know how she does, and thanks for asking me to join in the prayer efforts for this precious little one.

Lots of total strangers are in love with Ava . . . it's awesome to see God working!

Ava has lots of prayer warriors lifting her up to our heavenly Father! There's no doubt in my mind that she's going to be okay! We love you guys.

Love,
Kim

CHAPTER 7

-----ᨓᨓᨓ-----

Miracles

Ava is keeping the doctors busy. The blood clot in her abdomen had decreased in size on two sonograms yesterday. We were hopeful that the medicine administered to break it up, tissue plasminogen activator (TPA), was working. In the middle of the night, the clot broke off a small piece and lodged somewhere in her right-leg knee area. Her foot was losing circulation and was cold and white. We prayed, my mom had her talk with Ava, and we waited.

Miraculously, the blood clot was gone at the 6:00 a.m. sonogram, and her little right foot was warm, pink, and moving around.

The plan for the day was to rest, get her blood levels corrected, and prepare for repair surgery in the next two to five days. As I was sitting next to Ava's bed, Dr. Thomas came in and stood next to me. "Remember when we met I told you and Todd I would be direct and honest with you concerning Ava's condition and care," he said. "Ava has a six-millimeter spot on her brain that's bleeding." I did not know how to respond. I just held Ava's little hand.

Bleeding is a risk of being on ECMO because they have to use blood thinners to circulate the blood in and out of the ECMO circuit. It also could have been from the TPA clot-buster medication, but that was a life threatening issue yesterday so it had to be done. A doctor immediately administered a drug that can slow down and possibly even stop the bleeding in the brain. We won't know until results come back from another brain sonogram at 6:00 p.m. tonight. We need another miracle from above to work with Ava's strength, the medicine, and the doctor's knowledge to get her through this next battle. She

17

has to make it through this so she can have her repair surgery. She *has* to get to the point of the beginning of her recovery.

If the bleeding progresses, she will have to come off ECMO, as early as tonight, so she can stop taking the blood thinners. If she comes off ECMO, she will have to survive on her current lung capacity. We did get the good news that her lungs and heart have seemed to react positively to this rest provided by ECMO.

The 6:00 p.m. brain sonogram did show growth, which was expected since we did not start the drug to stop the bleeding until 2:00 p.m. However, the growth was very small, and Dr. Thomas was relieved, as were we. Another sonogram will be done at 6:00 a.m. If it shows no progression of bleeding, then that should open a window of opportunity for surgery. Surgery could be done as early as tomorrow midmorning. Ava will ultimately decide when it's time. She's resting very peacefully now and has continued to amaze us with her will to fight these battles. Six days old, and she's preparing for her second surgery.

No one will ever have to remind me we have a miracle child. And I don't know how we will ever thank all the people who have touched our lives with love, support, and prayer.

CHAPTER 8

Repair Surgery Scheduled, Again

The morning sonogram came back with good results. The bleeding in her brain has stopped and is showing signs of decreasing in size. Team Ava is in the process of changing her room into an operating room. The surgery should start by 3:00 p.m. and last about two hours.

Please pray for Ava, her doctors, surgeons, and nurses.

Guestbook entries:

God be with you.

Dr. Tommy

~

Hey Jen,

Thank you so much for the pictures and the updates. I have been following them closely and have been updating my staff and team as well! Ava was born on our first day of practice and was the topic of my "Cardinal's Nest" discussion (where we go around and say one good thing that happened that day). I can't wait for practice today to tell my players how she made it through the blood clot challenge and is now resting and ready for surgery.

Also, I just wanted to let you know you aren't alone on this roller coaster ride, and I wish I could be there in person to support you, Ava, and the whole family. Melissa, I, and the North Central basketball program are all thinking about you and praying for Ava's recovery!

Hang in there!

Michelle

~

I'm a friend of Stephanie Studdard's and just wanted to tell you how much I'm praying for Ava. I am *so* sorry that you and she have to be going through this. For Ava I'm praying for healing, and for you I'm praying for comfort, peace, and strength that only comes from God.

Warmest regards,
Allison

CHAPTER 9

———⚬⚬⚬———

Successful Surgery

Our family took up most of the waiting room. Sitting next to me were Todd and my parents. My sister, twin nieces, cousins, aunts, and uncles all sat in a peaceful silence, prayed, and waited. I remembered an e-mail from my best friend in response to finding out about Ava's condition before she was born: "I have so much faith about this: she is going to be *fine*, and you will laugh with her one day about all the drama her debut created. Please know I am *constantly* thinking of you."

I stared out of the twelfth-floor window across the Dallas skyline and saw Methodist Central Hospital, where I was born thirty-five years ago—where up until one month ago I thought Ava would be born. Months of planning and preparing for her birth did not include this, but I was thankful to be right where I was sitting. Glancing back across the room at my family, I realized how blessed I am to have them right by my side.

The nurses came through the door with smiles on their faces. They are sewing Ava's little tummy up now, and we should be talking to the surgeons soon to learn the details of the procedure. Many thanks to everyone for all of your support!

Okay, the surgeons just left. They said the surgery went exceptionally well. All of her organs were moved down, and her diaphragm was repaired with the patch. There's not enough room in her tummy for her newly placed organs, so there's another patch at the wound sight. That patch will be removed later once her skin stretches. Team Ava will watch her recovery hour by hour for the next several days. She will remain on ECMO to help in recovery, and we really do not know for how long. It could be days to several more weeks.

There is still a long road ahead for recovery. There are risks and many potential complications. But now Ava can come out of her corner of the ring and really start fighting.

Guestbook entries:

> That is wonderful news! So happy to hear that the surgery went so well! What a strong baby and even stronger parents! I know she will continue to fight! Give amazing Ava a kiss from Aunt Carmel!
>
> Carrie

~

> Here's hoping for a few uneventful days with little happening other than the love among you, Todd, and Ava growing.
>
> Duke

~

> The courage of that little girl and the strength you and Todd are showing humbles us. Ava is in our thoughts and prayers. She is obviously surrounded by love both at her bedside and far away. We will continue to pray for her and your family. She inspires us all.
>
> Love,
> Toni

Surgery Celebration

**Grandpa Jack, Cousin Kim, Grandma Karen,
Aunt Becky and Aunt Kristi celebrate a successful
repair surgery.**

CHAPTER 10

※

Rest and Recover

If I could dress Ava up for Halloween, she'd definitely be Wonder Woman. Ava's doctor referred to her as being "rock solid" during surgery. The first crucial twenty-four hours post-surgery were stable. I can tell she's in more pain today because of the surgery, and she became agitated easily during hourly vital signs testing. She did get a new ECMO machine because the circuit was clotting. That switch took two hours to prime and prep the new machine and only one minute to swap them out. She was off ECMO during the swap and did well. A head sonogram confirmed the bleeding in her brain has stopped; the chest x-ray did not show any clots.

Ava has had a stable few days and nights which is exactly what her heart and lungs need. The next step is to evaluate her pulmonary arterial hypertension (PAH). This is something we knew she had all along, but stabilization and repair surgery were priorities. PAH is abnormally high blood pressure in the arties of the lungs. It makes the right side of the heart work harder than normal. There is a part of her heart they are trying to evaluate through echocardiograms (like a sonogram) to see where the PAH may be stemming from. PAH is something CDH babies are born with, stemming from underdeveloped lung tissue and their hearts being pushed to the right side of their bodies. Now that she's got more space in her chest cavity, her doctors can start to evaluate how well her heart and lungs function together.

I feel good that we are moving down this list of hurdles since it's a lengthy one. The doctors still are not time-lining anything, so we are taking things day by day. They round every morning at 9:00

a.m. so we get a new plan each day. At rounds we listen intently to her doctors, nurses, respiratory therapists, and ECMO specialists report on the last twenty-four hours and the plan for the next.

We have had family rotating in from out of town help us keep up with things. My aunts and uncles have been taking care of my parents' house, picking up the twins from school, feeding us, and being here emotionally for us. It's been such a blessing. Todd and I are getting more sleep, with the help of my superwoman mom. Dad is on call for food and always here for support. My family is awesome, and Todd and I can't say thanks enough to them!

Well, I'm sitting in Ava's room. Her numbers are stable and she looks like an angel. We are in the middle of shift change, so I better go meet the wonderful nurses who will take care of her today. We have lots of the same ones, and they've really become attached to her! I'm going to stand by her bed and wait for her to open her eyes so I can sing "good morning to you" to her. Please keep Ava in your thoughts and prayers. Many thanks to everyone! *We* love you!

Guestbook entries:

> I am so happy to hear that "superwoman" is responding well to surgery! Now more than ever, I have no doubt in my mind that *prayer works*! So we are going to keep on praying for her so she can soon get well and finally go home to her loving family!!
>
> Erika

~

Jennifer:

> I praise God and give Him all of the glory for her continued healing! I pray that He continues to give her strength and to bless her and her family with peace and comfort. Love to all of you.
>
> Carla

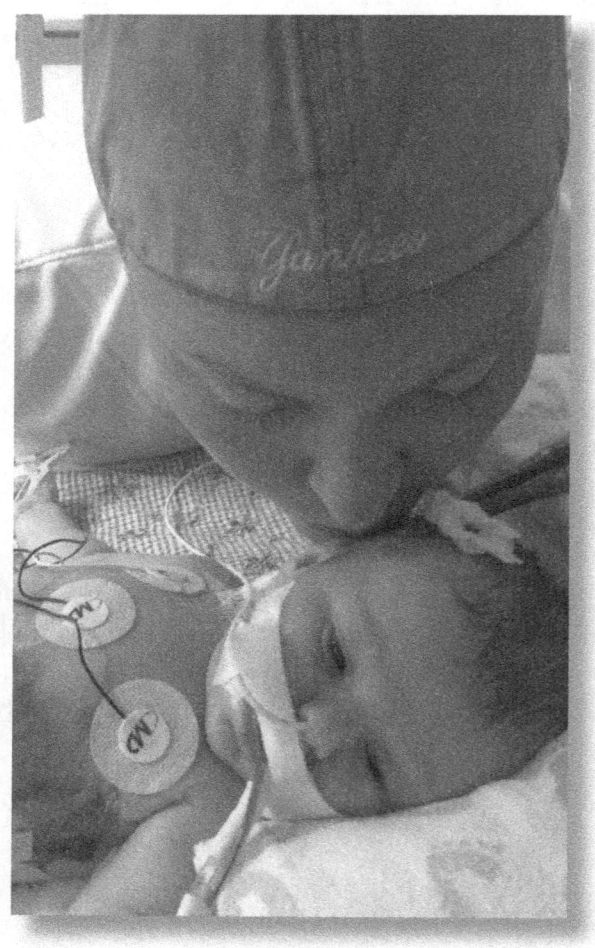

Daddy's Kisses

A sweet kiss from Daddy to Ava.

CHAPTER 11

Day 14

Ava continues to have fairly stable days and nights. She's got a few numbers they are working on with different medications and ECMO flows to try to stabilize. Over the past few days, her chest x-rays have shown her right lung (her good one) to have collapsed. It's a very fragile balance to keep it open with gentle ventilation since ECMO does her lung function for her. They have tried to wean her ECMO flow down several times but she's not tolerating it because of her collapsed lung and PAH. Currently, her ECMO is set at 120, with 130 being the highest support and 30 being the lowest. We have to get that right lung opened in order to progress forward with weaning, but the doctors are saying it's a very slow process. They have chest x-rays scheduled for every twelve hours, but it could be several days before they show any improvement.

The plan for the weekend is to let her rest. We had a very dramatic early morning on Wednesday. Her nurse woke me up at 3:00 a.m. to let me know there was a leak in the roof from the rain going right onto a machine that controls her kidneys. Before I could get off the couch, the lights in the room came on, and there were twenty doctors and nurses in the room preparing for us to evacuate to another room. It took all of them to move Ava and her machines inch by inch two rooms down. Dr. Thomas lead Team Ava very slowly as each person had their own responsibility on the short trip, which took over an hour. I stood in the background with tears running down my checks, scared and nervous.

Also, earlier that evening, as the nurses were shifting her on the bed, she slipped down and the cannulas in her neck moved slightly making the ECMO circuit cut in and out. They recovered quickly, but I think both those events really took a toll on Ava. Her numbers have fluctuated more since the move. The doctors have recommended minimal stimulation to allow her to rest and let the gentle ventilation work to open her lungs.

Ava continues to get her strength and will from your love, support, and prayers. She also got her own set of pink boxing gloves from her grandpa yesterday. I'm sure as soon as we can dress, her grandpa will order pink shorts and a robe to go with the gloves. She's our little fighter!

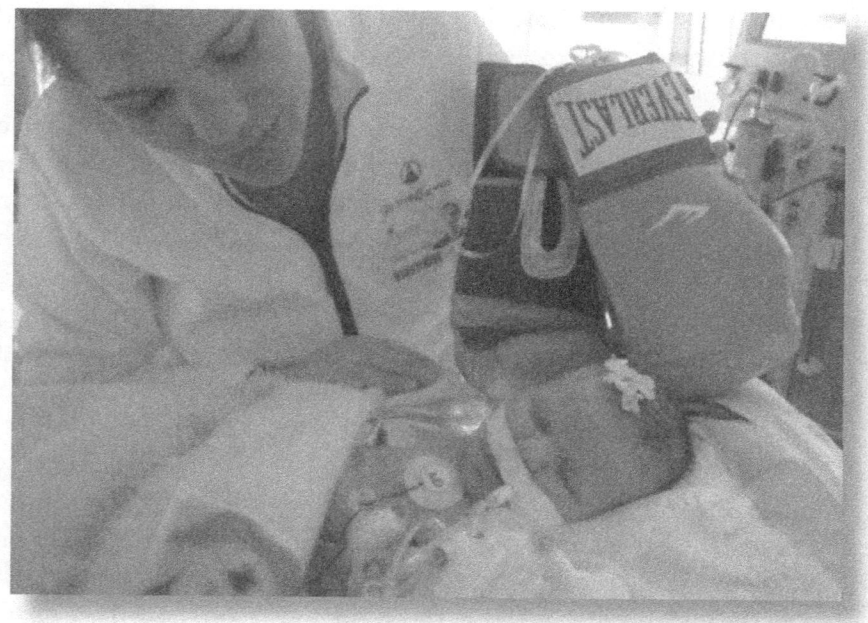

Ava's Gloves

Ava's pink boxing gloves from Grandpa hang in her room next to her bed.

CHAPTER 12

———∞∞∞———

Critically Stable

Ava continues to fight and has recruited a good portion of her right lung and even a little bit of her left lung! Great news! The doctors are pleased with her progress. They changed her ventilation to an oscillator which delivers small, short breaths of air into her lungs. Even though ECMO breathes for her, we still need her lungs to function in order to be successful in the weaning process (along with managing her PAH). Her kidneys are not functioning as well as before, but the doctors seem to believe once off ECMO, they will be fine. One doctor said he would like to set a goal of Friday for her to be weaned off. I was surprised he set a plan for further out than the next twenty-four hours—go, Ava!

One small step back is that she's contracted a cold but is showing no symptoms yet. My mom, Todd and I can still stay in her room but not too close to her bed. And anyone coming into her room has to wear gloves, masks, and a gown. So her ECMO doctor does not want any more visitors in her room until she's off ECMO. When I think about her condition as "critically stable," it makes sense that minimal stimulation is best for her so she can remain strong and rest. When I look at her, I do not see the tubes, wires, lines, and cannulas connecting her precious body to all the machines. I don't see a "critically stable" or "sick" baby. I see our beautiful little girl staring up at me saying she's fighting and going to be just fine. But I have to tell you, it breaks my heart that I can't scoop her up! When I do get the chance, I don't think I'll ever put her down!

Ava continues to rest and take small steps forward. She got another new ECMO machine yesterday (the third now) because the old one was developing blood clots, which are common. The procedure to transition to the new machine was smooth. Mom and I stood right outside the room and peeked through the window. It's a very intense process that requires precise timing as they move from one life support machine to another. They clamp the two cannulas, cut them, and then reattach them to the new machine. They cover Ava completely with drapes, and as the ECMO specialists were finishing up, Ava raised her right arm through the drapes which had everyone in the room smiling. It was like she was saying, "Hey docs, don't forget about me under here."

Todd and I enjoyed a nice evening with Ava. She had her eyes open for about an hour, and we talked, sang some lullabies, and read stories to her. She follows the pictures with her eyes, and is very alert. I think *Goodnight Moon* is her favorite book.

The doctors are back to day by day on ECMO to let her PAH resolve and lungs rest. It's been sixteen days since she's been on ECMO, and they are keeping her flows at full capacity until they try weaning again.

Ava and Todd are both asleep, so I think I'll try and join them in their sweet dreams. Good night. I will update you in another few days. We send our love and thanks to everyone!

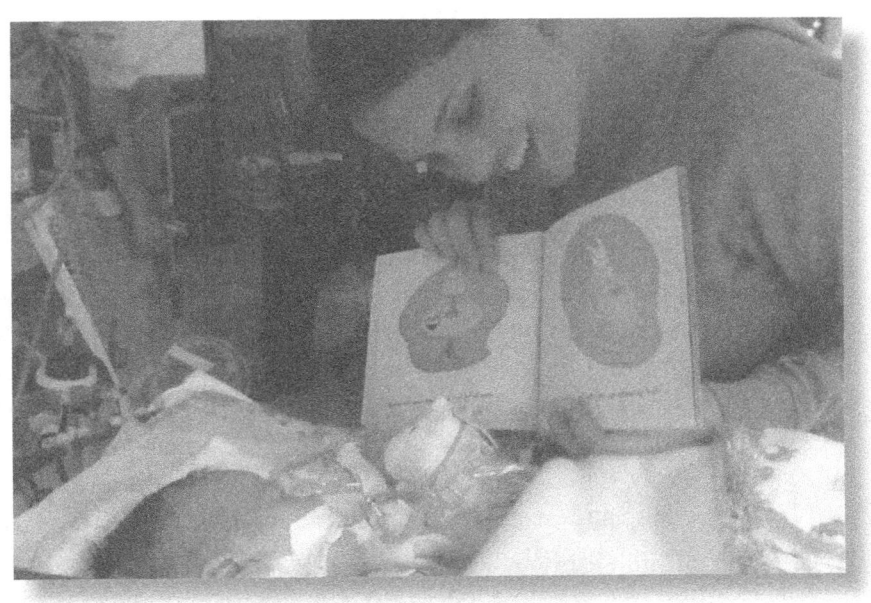

Reading to Ava

Mommy reading to Ava

CHAPTER 13

Holding Ava

I got to hold her today. I am tearing up just thinking about it. I got to hold my precious Ava today. When I came in this morning (thanks, Mom, for babysitting so I could stay at home with Todd), the lead ECMO specialist, Ralph, said they needed to change her bedding today. He said I could lift her off the bed while they swapped blankets and he held her cannulas in place. The cannulas are what connect her to ECMO. It was a one-two-three count by Ralph, and three weeks after Ava was born, I lifted her off her bed. I've had many happy tears today! By the way, she's solid and seems to be at least eight pounds!

We have officially started the weaning process. We started it yesterday, so it's been over twenty-four hours, and Ava is tolerating it well. Her numbers have stayed steady; the doctors are pleased. Her kidneys and bowels are still quiet, but they seem to think they will be fine once off ECMO. Her ECMO flow is currently at seventy-five cubic centimeters per kilo, and once she gets to thirty, she will be idle. They will clamp the cannulas to see how well she tolerates just being on the oscillator. When she passes that test (we all know she will), her surgeons will perform surgery to decannulate.

I am excited, nervous, and thankful we are at this point. Team Ava is too! I will keep you updated over the weekend.

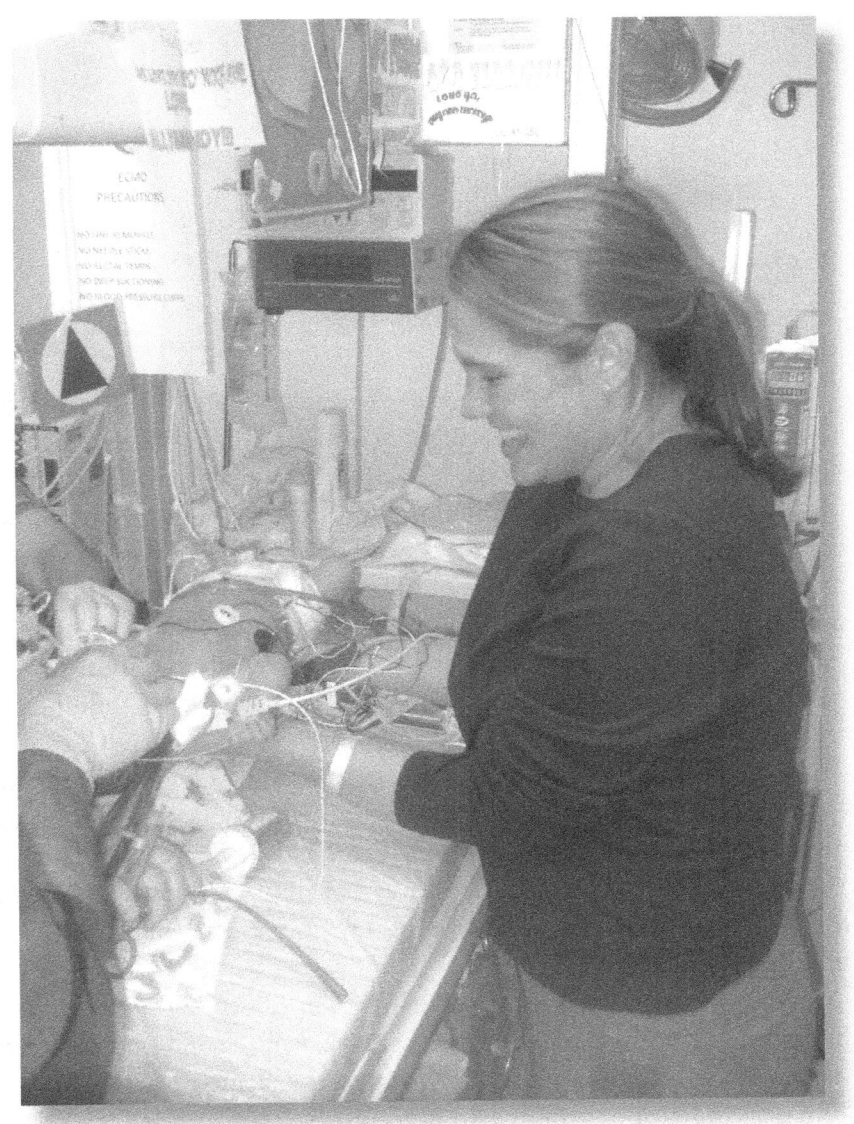

Holding Ava

CHAPTER 14

———— ∞ ————

Ava's Numbers

We had a restful weekend. Ava got down to sixty cc per kilo on her ECMO flows on Friday night. They gave her a day to rest on full capacity flows on Saturday and then started weaning her again yesterday. They are gradually taking the flows back down, and we are currently at 60 (as low as 50 earlier). Bringing the flows down is a balancing act and takes time. Going back up and down again is okay and allows Ava to adjust on her own time. She's still driving the bus!

I find myself staring, almost obsessing, over her numbers. The oxygen levels, blood pressure, heart rate, and ECMO flows are changing every minute. They continuously increase and decrease depending on medications, on flows, on if she's agitated, and so forth. I remember Shawn Studdard telling me the numbers on her monitor show an overall picture when analyzed all together. He said to try and not worry minute to minute over her numbers, but here I sit on the couch in her room as she sleeps, praying and hoping for all the numbers to be right.

We are back to our original doctor, Dr. Thomas, for two weeks. He rounded with Dr. Kerney, who took care of her the past two weeks, but still wants another day to become acclimated to her again. The plan today and tonight is to hold steady at lower flows. Her chest x-ray today showed more lung opened on both right and left. The head sonogram this week came back normal. The kidney sonogram showed good blood flow, which hopefully is a positive sign that her kidneys will kick in again once off ECMO.

As we get closer to decannulation (going off ECMO), I anticipate more hour-to-hour changes. I think she's resting up for the next big step, lacing up her gloves, and getting ready to breathe on her own.

Guestbook entries:

> We will keep the prayers going for our little angel. I am happy you have family there for you. We are close in spirit as you know. God continues to bless you with these little miracles
>
> Love, Angeline

~

> You are in our thoughts and prayers that everything will go well with Ava. We pray for strength for Ava, courage for her family, and a guiding hand with her medical team.
>
> Love,
> Judy and Bob Hamlet
> Shawn's aunt and uncle
> Kamryn's great-aunt and -uncle

CHAPTER 15

Ava's Signs

Ava has had a rough few days. She got her fourth ECMO and CVVH machines on Tuesday afternoon. She did great during the one-minute swap, but the following twenty-four hours were hard for her. She was not her bright-eyed, alert self. She was uncomfortable, agitated, and needed more pain and sedation medication. Even when she was sleeping, she was not comfortable. We were told that changing machines can take a toll on Ava's system since its running new blood through new lines and tubes that are not primed with her medication. However, the two times before, she bounced back within a few hours.

Ava's medications are set up on automatic dispensers and are timed depending on the dose and medication. A harsh reality that my head has accepted but breaks my heart is that Ava is on pain medication that is as strong and addictive as heroine. "A necessary evil" is one way a doctor explained it to me. If she's uncomfortable and agitated, the nurse has the option to give her an additional "bolus" of pain mediation each hour. I try to calm her down by softly singing to her and rubbing her forehead. I dim the lights, close the door, and play soft music. From the beginning of this journey, I told myself I would not cry in front of Ava; I have to stay strong for my little girl. When I see tears developing in her eyes and then running down her face, it's almost impossible to hold mine back. She opened her mouth, but because of the breathing tube, no sound came out. As I watched her silently cry, the nurse suggested a bolus will help calm her down. Heartbroken and helpless, I stayed next to Ava's bed while she received eight additional boluses throughout the night.

The next morning in rounds, Todd and I expressed our concerns and that I felt Ava was trying to tell us something was wrong. The doctors noticed a difference in her clinically also. As a precautionary treatment, they started her on two general antibiotics. They drew blood and mucus from her lungs to test for infections. It takes a minimum of forty-eight hours to see any infectious growth. These machines control her body temperature, so we cannot use that as an indicator for infection. Her white blood cell count is normal, which is a good sign of no infection, and her pressures have been stable. But we have to be patient and pray that there are no serious infections and that she does not become septic. She does look better today and is resting peacefully.

We have known that there are risks for infections with being on ECMO, having numerous lines into her tiny body, and just being a newborn baby. We also know that she's a fighter and has many angels looking over her. Just a little ride down the roller coaster; I'm sure those tests will come back negative. Go, Ava, go!

Plan for the next twenty-four hours: Keep a close watch for any clinical signs of distress (they do this always, everyday, regardless); start a medication which should help her PAH; and test lower ECMO flows (right now she's at eighty-three).

CHAPTER 16

—⊷⊶⊷—

Day 29

Ava has been cleared for any bronchial or viral infections, but we are still patiently waiting to see about any blood infections.

At rounds today her doctors are concerned about of her distended tummy, which indicates that her intestines may have a fungal infection called necrotizing enterocolitis (NEC); so they are starting another precautionary antibiotic. Dr. Kordy, who leads rounds, immediately ordered Ava's feeds to stop as soon as NEC was mentioned. The nurse continued to listen as Dr. Kordy continued with stats. I knew this condition was very serious when Dr. Kordy stopped midsentence to reiterate and ask again to have her feeds stopped, not after rounds but right now. Radiology is reading her morning stomach x-ray to look for any signs of NEC. I was disappointed that she had to stop getting my breast milk, knowing that was the best nutrition for her, but I know it was necessary. Two numbers that are monitored by ECMO-reads are ranging out of normal, one being her hemoglobin count. They want to eliminate the possibility of a brain hemorrhage developing, so they are doing a head sonogram right now to check. NEC can be serious and something Ava's little body may not tolerate. Team Ava seems very concerned, which always has us even more nervous.

Last night I was by Ava's bed, watching her sleep. Around midnight the on-call doctors do 'mini-rounds' on each patient in the NICU. I was listening to them talk about Ava in the hallway and overheard the word *sepsis* in their conversation. I was scared but did not recognize the doctor and did not ask him to clarify. Todd was at home with our son, Jason, so I called him with my concern. "Todd, what does sepsis mean?" He replied, "Who said that, Jennifer? Being septic can be fatal; it means you have an infection in your blood." I said, "They did not say *septic*, they said *sepsis*." As he told me it meant the same thing, I could sense a grave and scared feeling coming from the other end of the line. "Put the nurse on the phone or go get the doctor. We need to know if Ava's become septic." I hung up with Todd and asked the nurse to page the doctor. He arrived momentarily and told me Ava could possibly be septic but time would tell.

At normal rounds the next morning, I asked Dr. Thomas and Team Ava about sepsis. Yes, Ava is showing signs of an internal infection, but we have to wait for test results and watch her closely until we can confirm either way. All of these concerns have them going back up on her ECMO flows until they can be eliminated. If she does have an infection and is possibly septic, she needs to fight that fight and not use her strength for weaning.

Sweet Ava, please get some rest and let all these things the doctors are worried about go away! Keep on fighting, and we'll keep on praying, hoping, and loving on you.

CHAPTER 17

---∞∞∞---

Twenty-Four Hours Later, We Exhale

Ava has overcome, again! Most of the signs are pointing toward *not* having a blood infection or NEC (infection of the bowels): the white blood count is normal, her tummy is less distended and not as tender, and she had a stable night of stats. Dr. Thomas said he will continue the antibiotics to be safe and watch the cultures for another few days for bacteria growth. He said she probably was not tolerating higher amounts of feeds and he would not restart those until off ECMO. *No problem, I will keep on pumping and freezing and will have months' worth of milk built up for you when you come home. We bought a deep freeze just for you and your milk because Nancy told me they are running out of room here.*

So we are back on course. We will concentrate on weaning, slowly, as they titrate up on floane (the drug that will help decrease her PAH). Ava will determine the timeline. We had a mommy-daughter talk this morning about showing the doctors how well she can manage her PAH (pulmonary hypertension) and wean off ECMO.

Remember Book A, Ava? Let's write the next chapter about weaning off ECMO successfully. Be strong and fight. We'll be right by your side, sweet girl.

Dear Ava,

You have touched so many lives and warmed so many hearts since you were born. And even though you are only four weeks and three days old, you have faced and overcome so many challenges just to stay alive. You are a true fighter. I am so proud to be your mommy.

It's time, baby girl, to lace those gloves up tight and face your next challenge. Dr. Thomas said you can't take ECMO to kindergarten, so it's time to show him you do not need that big machine anymore. He said they were going to push you this week. Help that medicine fight your PAH away and let your lungs breathe. These next few days will be hard for you, and I wish I could do it for you. But you know we are right next to you, holding your little hands and praying for your big life.

I thank God that He continues to give you the strength you need to keep fighting. You are our little miracle, our little fighter, our sweet Ava. I love you more than any words will ever be able to describe.

Love,
Mommy

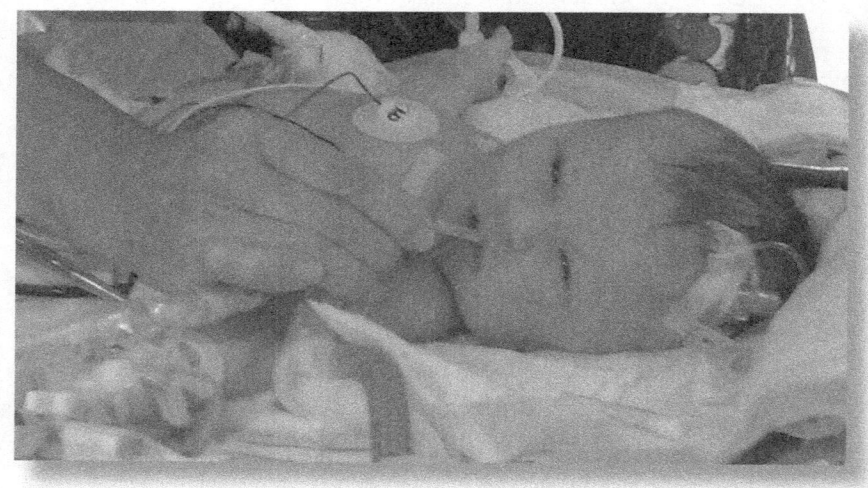

Ava's Smile

Nurse Nancy changed Ava's dressing on her
breathing tube and Mommy was able to snap a
picture of her beautiful smile.

Chapter 18

Thanksgiving Eve

Dear Family and Friends,

This is going to be one of the hardest journal entries to write as I recap today's rounds with you. Todd and I had a reality check with Dr. Thomas this morning. When we first met him, he told us we are in this together and he will be honest and open on the medical treatment and progress of Ava. He said that "we are medically out of options."

We have known that with CDH, one of the most serious issues is pulmonary hypertension (PAH). It took us a few weeks to get to this point of aggressively treating it. Going on ECMO and getting her repair surgery done were first priorities. Her PAH is severe. She's on six medications to help treat and manage it. One of the medications is at its maximum. One looks like it's getting to the maximum with her pressures and side effects. Two were just started today. She's been on ECMO for thirty-one days. I have reached out to the close-knit CDH community to see if any other babies have been on ECMO this long. Many parents have responded, but I think Ava may set a record for the number of days for an infant. Dr. Thomas said we are venturing into uncharted territory. They are treating her more aggressively than any other CDH cases they have had. (Well, I know that's because she's the strongest fighting baby they have seen.) He's consulting with colleagues around the world about further treatment for Ava. Todd asked Dr. Thomas today if he's still hopeful. He said, "Yes, we *hope* those medications will work."

Let us all pray for another miracle. Let us hold on to that hope that has got all of us, including Ava, this far. Let our sweet Ava fight that PAH away and use her will that God blessed her with to get through this next challenge.

Many thanks from our family to yours for your prayers, love, and support. Happy Thanksgiving! We are so very thankful for our family and friends.

Love,
Jennifer and Todd

CHAPTER 19

---⊗⊗⊗---

"Onward We Go"

To all of Ava's supporters,

We are thankful and overwhelmed with the size of this wonderful network.

In rounds yesterday, Dr. Thomas said he stayed up most of the night before going over Ava's case. He decided to add epinephrine (adrenaline) to her list of medications. It almost acts with opposite effects, but on different parts of her cardiovascular system, as the other medications. I completely understand his logic in rounds (they draw pictures and answer questions) but getting that back to the keyboard is difficult. He is trying to manipulate her blood flow. Blood flow goes in the path of least resistance. Her lungs are super-resistant (PAH); so he's trying to make her body more resistant than her lungs so they get enough blood flow to ultimately wean off ECMO. Just know that we are still in uncharted territory, but we have experts from all over the world giving their input for Ava.

Dr. Chen, with whom we have developed a personal relationship, sat in our room last night and had a great talk with us. She has been a part of Team Ava from the beginning and knows her well. She knows Ava is capable of beating the odds and fighting battles. She said we just need to see improvement each day in order to continue in these uncharted waters. Improvement justifies keeping her on ECMO and continuing treatment.

I am happy to report that we have improvement. Her chest x-ray this morning showed less fluid, the doctors can hear better lung sounds, and her tummy is less distended. "Overall she's better, so onward we go" (exact words from Dr. Thomas).

This is all good news for now, but it is still a very long road we are going down; so please keep Ava in your prayers. Getting off ECMO will (believe it or not) be the first step down that long road.

Our prayers are being answered. Medicine and miracles are happening in this room. Ava is not only reading Book A but she's writing it. Thank you for your continued prayers and support. Sweet Ava would not be writing this book without you.

Love,
Jennifer and Todd

CHAPTER 20

Bidirectional Flow

Ava's 4:00 p.m. echo showed bidirectional flow of blood in her heart. Her heart is pumping blood into her lungs on its own! Dr. Thomas was on the phone with the head of ECMO department as another doctor stood by the echo technician. Normally, the technician does the sonogram and then sends it to radiology to read and report back to the doctor. The fastest we've had a report delivered from a sonogram or echogram was thirty minutes. However, this time, Team Ava stood on standby and watched the screen. Then Dr. Thomas declared, "We have bidirectional flow!" They all looked like they were ready to do cartwheels, and the excitement reached down the halls of the twelfth floor of PICU. This has never happened! She's making medical history. Dr. Kordy and Dr. Carrie (the cheerleading section of Team Ava) were close by and celebrating the great news.

Dr. Thomas's updated plan for the next 24 hours: She'll stay the course today and tonight. Tomorrow she will have a tube drain the rest of the fluid around her right lung. Then she'll come off ECMO. She's telling us she's ready.

You know it's a great day when you group hug with Team Ava.

Dear Sweet Ava,

You are the bravest little girl; we are all so very proud of you. I hope you are feeling better after all that fluid (eighty-five cubic centimeters, almost three ounces!) was drained off your lung. Your chest x-ray, after they drained the fluid, shows lots of great lung space! Your numbers have increased, and Team Ava is very happy with your progress.

The plan for today and tomorrow is to let your lungs recruit, rest, and wean off ECMO. Sounds good? Remember we are right here by your side. We'll be praying while you're reading and writing.

Go, Ava, go!

Love,
Mommy, Daddy, and Gaga

Guestbook entries:

Dear Ava,

Aunt Kristi is so proud of you! We love you very much! Keep fighting, baby girl! Show them how it's done!

Love,
Aunt Kristi

~

Dear Jennifer, Todd, and Baby Ava,

What an incredible little baby. We are so happy to read of every amazing milestone Ava is able to accomplish. Thankfully you are in the very best hospital with brilliant medical minds working tirelessly to help Ava win every battle and eventually win the war. There are so many people out here praying for you and your family.

Jennifer and Terry Williams
Madelyn
(Kamryn Hope's Aunt, Uncle, and Cousin)

~

Dear Precious Ava,

I continue to pray for you and your family, and God continues to answer our prayers. You are such a fighter. Continue the fight. I love your updates and pictures! I can't wait to see the picture of your mom, dad, grandma, grandpa all cuddling with you. You are definitely a gift from God. I will keep praying, and you keep fighting. Bless you.

Love,
Jani

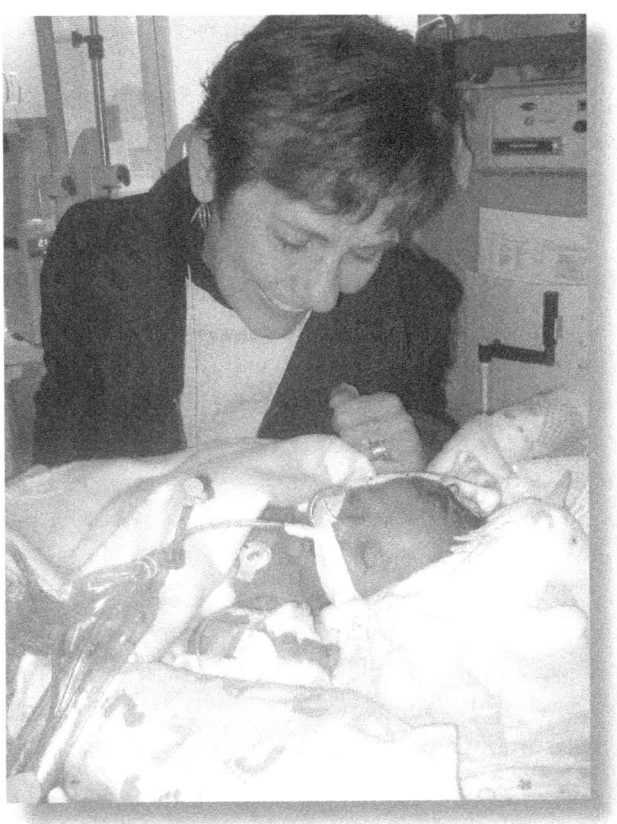

Grandma and Ava

CHAPTER 21

Baby Steps

Overall, Ava is doing great. Her lungs still need more recruiting. She will have several different treatments today to help break up any mucus plugs so they may extract them. This will ensure her lungs are at their fullest capacity when they aggressively wean. They will keep her at eighty (remember 30 is idle) today on her ECMO flows. Her numbers are great (heart rate, blood pressure, blood gases, O_2 saturation). She's almost ready.

Unfortunately, when they do start aggressively weaning, they may have to give her a paralytic to completely sedate her. This will optimize her chances for weaning and coming off ECMO. Please know that as I type out that my baby has to be paralyzed for hours, possibly days, I don't accept it. I mean, my brain accepts it but my heart is having a hard time. I understand pain and sedation drugs are necessary for Ava's comfort. And my whole body hurts when I see her hurting (we can't hear her cry, but we can see her crying).

Tomorrow is probably the day. I can't say for sure until after rounds, but I know we are getting close. I will mark it down as the first day sweet Ava lives off life support. Sure, she'll have breathing assistance from a ventilator, but she'll be a pro coming off that.

Okay, baby girl, rest up and let your lungs clear out. I love you.

Guestbook entries:

Dearest Ava,

We have been keeping up with your progress and praying for your speedy recovery. We know a little about what you and your parents are going through, because Kamryn Hope is our granddaughter, and as you know, she was born with CDH, too.

We want you to know that we will be with you in our thoughts and prayers tomorrow as they take away that big, scary ECMO.

You have touched our hearts because through all this, you have been such a big, brave girl. Please stay strong tomorrow and feel the love from all your new friends.

We look forward to hearing good news tomorrow. Give your parents our love. They've been very brave, too.

With all our love,
Carol and Joe

~

Baby Ava,

Keep fighting, sweet baby girl! I know you are strong, just like your mommy, and you can do it! I can't wait to see you again, and I know everyone here is looking forward to finally meeting you. Kelcie can't wait to play with you and teach you all she has learned about jewelry and shoes (your mommy's favorite things). We continue to pray for your strength and progress. God is watching over you. Keep those gloves laced up, Ava!

Love,
Aunt Carmel and the whole Hayes Family

~

We are so there with you—all the way—praying for the quickest, least painful getting there for Ava.

Anna and Larry

Chapter 22

Book A

Her right lung continues to improve and they are concentrating on getting full recruitment as they wean down her flows. She will have a bronchial tube with a camera and suction device attached go down her airway to look for any mucus plugs. If it looks clear, then they will have to do a computed tomography (CT) scan to see if there is any additional fluid to drain. Team Ava wants to optimize her right lung before getting down to lower ECMO flows.

Assuming her lung continues to recruit, they will lower the flows by ten cubic centimeters each day. The goal today is to get down to seventy. She will not have to have paralytic sedation until her movement, and her being awake affects her numbers. She will let us know.

The last twenty-four hours, Ava has been happy, alert, and awake for songs, story time, and updates on Book A. Thanks to everyone for your continued love and prayers for baby Ava!

Guestbook entries:

> Jennifer, we are so thrilled to get the updates on Ava. The pictures that you send are beautiful. What a sweet little girl she is!
>
> I am so glad that things are going well. Somehow I knew they would.
>
> You and Ava will forever be in our prayers.
>
> Pam

~

Jennifer: Ava is beautiful and quite the fighter. Praying for healing and encouragement for her and strength and peace for you and Todd. May you feel God's hand on you today.

Blessings,
Laura (Leftwich) Pulis

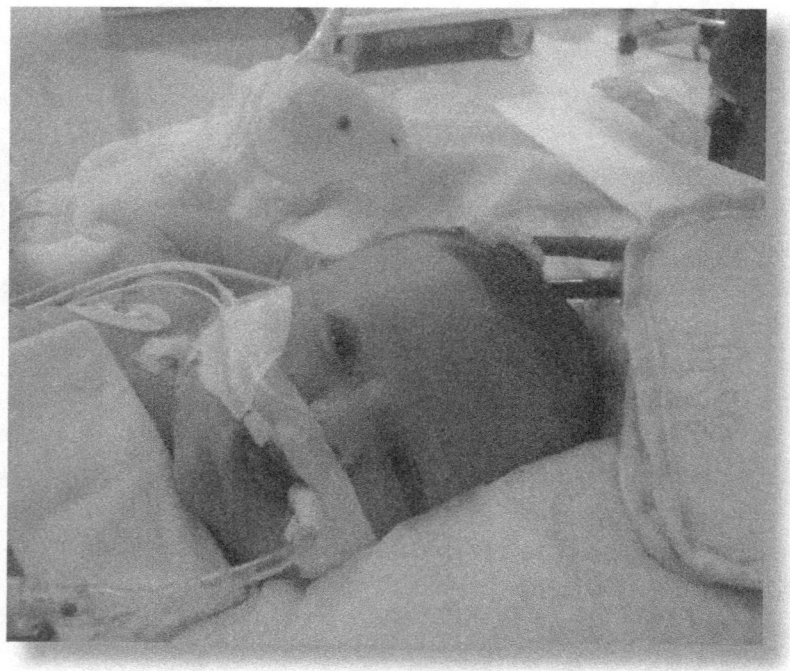

Sweet Ava

CHAPTER 23

---ꙮ---

Day 40

Ava had a challenging day. Yesterday afternoon, they had to change her ET tube (breathing tube) to a larger one to accommodate the bronchial tube with the camera. That was traumatic. Last night she was very agitated and in pain. Then today they actually did the bronchial scan. That, too, was traumatic. They did not see or remove much mucus, but it did show bleeding throughout her right lung. Bleeding is a side effect of being on ECMO because they have to run heparin (blood thinner) through the circuit. They can fix the bleeding with platelets and coagulates.

Team Ava also did an echo on her heart today to see the function of her four pulmonary ventricles. They are functioning but not to their expectations. Her heart rate has been elevated since last night.

During the last twenty-four hours, they had to go up on her ECMO flows to support her while enduring these procedures. The plan is to keep her at eighty cubic centimeters this evening. Tomorrow they may do the CT scan, but that does require her and her entourage of equipment to go to another floor. Dr. Chen said they would weigh the risks versus benefits on the CT scan in the morning. Either way, it sounds like the weaning will continue tomorrow.

Please keep Ava in your thoughts and prayers as she continues the weaning process. We are grateful for all of your support.

Guestbook entries:

Ava,

We are praying for you, sweet girl. We are so proud of all the progress you've made! Keep it up, and soon you will be able to be in your momma's arms and loving every minute of it. I can't wait to see that picture. Your momma is the most amazing and strongest person I know. I can't wait to meet you and give you a hug and kiss, but until then, know that the entire Watt family loves you and is sending you so much love! Your cousin Ryan loves watching your YouTube video. He asks to see "baby" all the time.

I pray every day that God watches over you and that He guides the doctors and nurses to take care of you the best way possible. You are proof that God does still perform miracles on earth.

You keep showing them how strong you are! You are a fighter!

Love you all,
Michelle, Joe, Alyssa, Alex, Sean, and Ryan

~

My dear sweet, precious Ava,

You have some challenging days ahead, but we know that you are ready. Know that God is with you and helping you every step of the way. You are such a brave little girl, and we are so proud of you. So many people love you and can't wait for you to be home. Lace up those gloves and stay strong. You'll soon be home with all the people who love you. Grandma and Grandpa love you more than words can say, and we can't wait to hold you in our arms.

Love forever,
Grandma

Dear Jennifer,

I am so proud of you. You have stayed so strong for Ava. You are the best mommy in the world. I'll be right by your side while Ava is fighting this next battle. We can do this together.

Love,
Mom

CHAPTER 24

———∞∞∞———

A Small Bump in the Road

Ava is still battling the bleeding in the lung, which shows being collapsed again on this morning's x-ray. The respiratory therapist (RT) comes by twice an hour to suction fluid and clean out her breathing tube. I pray every time there's no more blood. The RT today is a cheerleader on Team Ava, and we just look at each other in silence as we watch blood being extracted from her breathing tube. Her ECMO circuit is clotting again from the continual addition of blood products. So she will get her fifth new circuit today, which will hopefully help stop the bleeding, and then we can go back to recruiting her right lung.

She's resting peacefully now and is absolutely beautiful! I know she's still fighting. She will clench her fists and move her little arms around when the doctors don't warm their stethoscope or cover her sweet eyes before turning on the bright lights. She keeps a firm grip on our fingers even after she falls asleep. That grip gives me hope, and I know our baby girl is still fighting.

I know the news today is a small step back. Ava is getting ready to take a few big steps forward. Please keep praying and never give up hoping. Here are a few videos that will hopefully make your heart smile. You tube links:

http://www.youtube.com/watch?v=Zmqqyi6ux6c
http://www.youtube.com/watch?v=AR_i-L7VeN8

Guestbook entries:

Ava and family: It feels like my heart misses a beat each time I receive an e-mail indication that there is a new journal entry on your CaringBridge page. I say a quick prayer and take a deep breath before opening the page, hoping and hoping that it will be continued positive news. Ava, you truly are a miracle baby who is writing new chapters in Book A that no one could have imagined. Be strong and continue to heal and grow. Odds are meant to be beaten, and you are the one to do it. Keep it going, big girl!

Sharon High

~

You are so right to hold tight to hope. Kamryn's middle name is Hope, and she clung to that as we all did while she fought. Ava is a fighter, too. You can see it in the way she listens to your soothing voice and watches your movements in spite of it all. This roller coaster ride is very difficult, and I remember talking to Kamryn and urging her to fight. To look at her now, you would never know the battle her little body fought. Ava will fight *just as hard*, and I pray that God speeds the time it takes for her to emerge free from ECMO. You are so positive, and that is half the battle. Blessings upon all of you!

Gammy Studdard

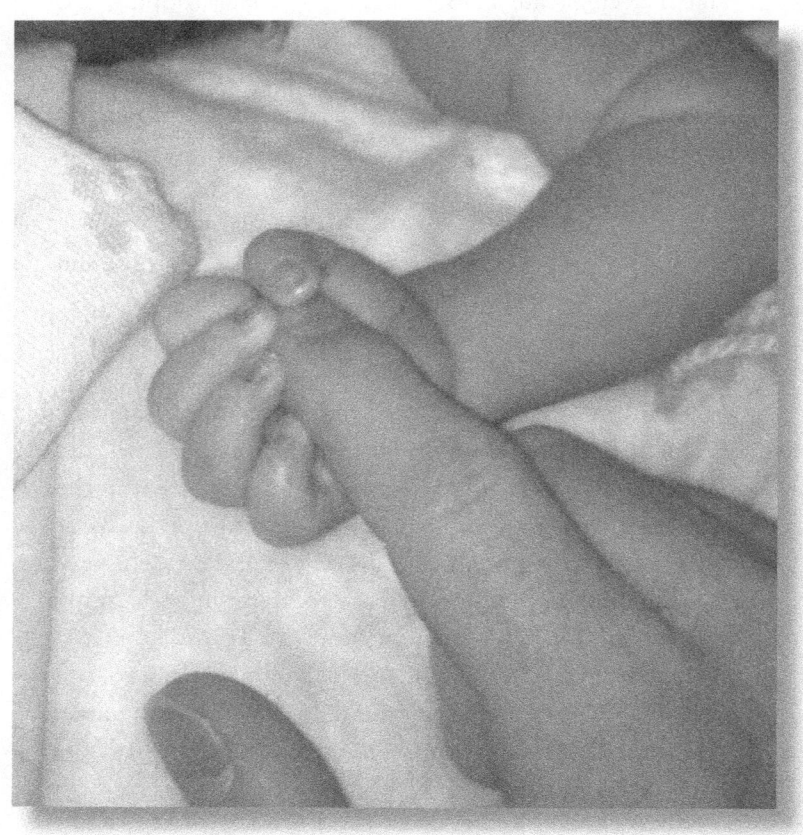

A Firm Grip

Ava holding her Daddy's finger tight.

CHAPTER 25

Holding Our Breath

Ava's new ECMO circuit is suiting her well. Her heart rate has leveled down to the 150 range. Her saturation levels are higher than they have been in the past few days, which is a good sign. She's a pro, and my mom and I have learned to hold our breath for as long as the switch takes. Last night it was one minute and five seconds.

Dr. Chen and Dr. Fischer (her colleague) spoke to us before rounds this morning. Yes, her lung is still bleeding, but it can take days for hemorrhages to subside. Yes, this is probably related to her severe PAH. But, most of all, *yes*, Ava is a miracle child from God. These two surgeons sat with us and reflected on the past forty-one days. Dr. Fischer said Ava was a miracle because of what she has already overcome.

We are hoping and praying that by Sunday, the bleeding has stopped and her lung has recruited so that we can begin weaning.

Again, thank you to everyone for your support and prayers. We can feel the love in her room. Your comments, e-mails, texts, phone calls, and visits all mean very much to our family.

CHAPTER 26

Six Weeks Old!

Ava has not had any more blood come up her ET tube since yesterday. We believe the bleeding has stopped or is pretty darn close to stopping. They adjusted a few settings on her oscillator to help recruit her right lung. We hope to see improvement on tomorrow morning's chest x-ray.

We have become friends with the family of the little boy, Sterling, who is next door to Ava. There is a window between the rooms that we keep open to share music and check in on each other. Sterling, who is just three years old, is on ECMO, too, and we are able to share our fears and support each other as our babies endure each day. Sterling accidently drank tiki oil at a family get-together a few weeks ago. It was in a container that resembled a water bottle, and within seconds, the poison consumed his lungs. Sterling and Ava are fighting together. Sterling's grandma, Tiffany, is the twelfth floor's prayer leader. She's very positive and helps keep our spirits up. Sometimes I come back from eating or taking a walk outside and find "Auntie Tiffany" by Ava's bed praying for her. I told her this morning that Ava's bleeding has stopped, and she said, "We'll keep sending the prayers up to send the blessings down!"

Guestbook entries:

Dear Jennifer, Todd, and Jason,

This is Linda (Luke, Lulu, and Buddy's new friend). I just read your journal of precious miracle baby Ava. It's a wonderful heartfelt story that I will use to follow Ava's journey. My thoughts and prayers are with you and your family. I pray for Ava's continued huge leaps over the hurdles. I also pray for your strength and comfort and continued miracles of wisdom performed by Team Ava. Today is better than yesterday, and tomorrow will be better than today. I'm thankful for being brought into your lives.

Linda Dunn
[Our new dog walker and friend we hired to take care of our three dogs while Ava is in the hospital.]

~

Dear Sweet Ava,

I'm praying for you with all the faith in my heart. I know you are a fighter; you are strong and full of life. You have overcome so many obstacles, so I know you will overcome it all. I believe in miracles, and you are a true miracle, and I know you will surprise us all.

I love you, sweet little Ava; can't wait to hold you and watch you grow.

Love always,
Nancy Escobar

CHAPTER 27

There She Goes, Again!

She's done it again—wowed the doctors with her chest x-ray! Her right lung has air in the lower lobe, and we hope to get more recruited in the next twenty-four hours. That's our plan for the day. Rest and recruit. They mentioned starting to wean her tomorrow, but we'll see how the lung looks, first.

I hope everyone has a wonderful weekend. Give your loved ones hugs and kisses from Ava. We all appreciate your love and prayers.

Guestbook entries:

> You have a real strong-willed girl on your hands. This is such great news. Miracles still happen.
>
> Bitsey Loy

~

> Oh, those chubby little feet on today's update! As soon as all these things are taken care of, she'll be up and running—literally. Love her!
>
> David and Kedra Sugg

~

So glad for the great news.

Anna and Larry

~

Dear God,

I stand in awe as I watch You perform one miracle after another. Thanks so much for hearing the prayers of your children! I know that You are the reason we can celebrate the progress Ava is making, and I want to thank you and give you the praise for all that You have done in her life. Please continue to give the doctors the wisdom and insight as they make decisions regarding Ava's treatment, and give Ava the will and strength to continue fighting.

Give strength and comfort to Jen, Todd, Aunt Karen, and the rest of the family.

Help us not be anxious about anything, but in everything, by prayer and petition, with thanksgiving, present our requests to You.

Philippians 4:6

Gratefully yours,
Kim

———∞∞———

CHAPTER 28

Here We Go

Ava got her daily assignment early today! It's a big one that will require her heart and lungs to work hard. She has rested all week to prepare for this next challenge: Ava will begin weaning off ECMO today.

Ralph is "sitting pump" (that's ECMO lingo for who's in charge of Ava's machine today). Ralph is our favorite. I knew it was Sunday when Nancy came in at 6:30 a.m. She is Ava's nurse, always, on Sundays and Mondays. Nancy taught me how to be a mom in ICU. We love her. Team Ava is ready.

In rounds this morning

The window to wean is open. Her lung is open. Her kidneys are starting to function again. She is systemically ready. The doctors said they have maximized therapy for her PAH. Her PAH will ultimately determine how well she tolerates weaning. They will raise the oscillator settings to help support her lungs as they decrease the flows. Dr. Thomas said, "Ava will either tolerate it or not." The goal is to have her at idle (thirty cubic centimeters) by tomorrow. *I wonder if I can hold my breath for that long.*

After rounds, just me and Ava

I told Ava how proud we were of her. I asked her to lace up her gloves and team up with the medications to fight through her PAH. I told her we can get rid of ECMO on her time and to just let us know. I told her about Christmas and how her grandma said she will leave her tree up until she comes home. I told her God and His angels are in the room. I asked her to be brave.

From the moment she was born, she's fought for her life and overcome so many challenges: blot clots, a brain bleed, CDH repair surgery, possible sepsis, and bleeding in her lung. And through this all, she's stayed strong and brought so many people together to help keep up the fight.

Here *we* go, sweet Ava—all of us together. We are praying, loving, and hoping.

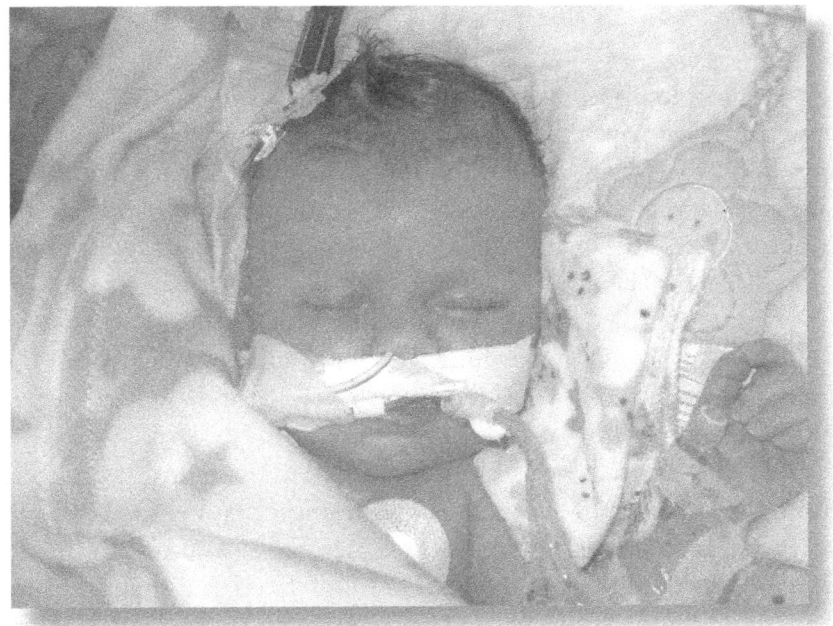

Beauty Shop with Nancy

Nancy paid special attention to little things like getting the goop out of Ava's hair after a head sonogram. She loved fixing Ava's hair.

CHAPTER 29

Coming off ECMO

We got down to seventy cubic centimeters on our ECMO flows yesterday. They did not want to push any further than that, because her blood gases were getting too low. Ava did great with her stats and was able to rest overnight. Today we wean again, do blood tests and monitor her stats.

Inhaling, exhaling.

We met with Ava's primary doctors, Dr. Chen, and nurse Nancy. Tomorrow is Ava's day to shine. They will take her off ECMO, and she will have her lungs supported by a ventilator. It will be her turn to pump blood into her lungs and breathe on her own.

Let me share a heartfelt story about the picture with today's post. Dr. Chen, Ava's surgeon, is also a photographer by hobby. She surprised Todd and me with precious pictures of Ava. Two of them are framed, one of her feet and one of her little hand. It is such a beautiful gesture of kindness, compassion, and love. Thank you, Dr. Chen, from the bottom of our hearts.

It is hard to find the words to express our gratitude to all the doctors and nurses on Team Ava. They have gone above and beyond for our little girl, and we will forever be thankful to them.

Ava will have a long list of thank-you notes to write when she gets home—doctors, surgeons, nurses, and especially her supporters who check in through her website daily. Please continue to pray for Ava tomorrow, her big day!

Guestbook entries:

I am praying for baby Ava! I will tell you that I do trust in God. I mean, wow, all these babies are fighters, but really, she has gone above and beyond the normal fight for these babies. I've never seen a baby do so well on ECMO for this long! I mean J. did great on it, but that was ten days! I am thanking God for what he is doing through her and with her. You all are so very blessed to be her parents, and this post just brought tears to my eyes. We love seeing her doing so well. I know she's still on ECMO, and most would say, "Well, that's *not* great," but no, she *is* doing great! What an amazing little girl you both have. May God just keep his hand on her as she fights this fight even harder today. Remember everyone that most babies do not come off ECMO at their first try, so do not get down if it's not tomorrow or today. I believe she can do it! We are going to be in Dallas in a couple weeks, and I pray that she'll be off ECMO and we can come and visit this most precious gift from God. We are thinking of her every day.

Candice Brooke Beal

P.S.: We love Ralph! He's such a "real" person that you can connect with easily. *We* are sending our love to you all!

~

Dear Ava,

Listen to your mommy. She wants you to keep fighting and be strong. We are all praying that you can come off ECMO soon. Take your time and keep up the fight. We are all praying for you. We can't wait to see your picture by Grandma's Christmas tree.

Love ya.
Jani

~

Jen and Todd,

I know we've never met, but I want you to know that I tear up every time I think about what you all are going through with your precious baby Ava. I know that you all are in God's hands, and there's no better place to be. I pray for your continued strength and courage daily. Always know someone is praying for you.

Love,
Liz

~

It was just over a year ago that our baby girl was also on floor twelve and had to come of ECMO. I remember Darla was sitting the pump that day. We hadn't been given much hope, and I remember being scared, but the Lord did something extraordinary for us that day and proved the odds wrong. We are praying now that our gracious God would again do something extraordinary for Ava, another precious baby girl on floor twelve—that tomorrow Ava would successfully come off ECMO and that her lungs and the vent would be strong enough to support her so she can continue to get stronger and stronger each day. We continue also to pray for the Lord's great peace for Ava's family, especially her mom and dad.

Susie Dutcher

Photographs by Dr. Chen

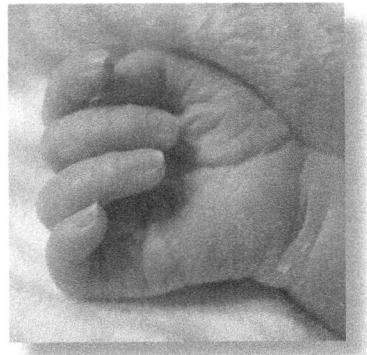

Ava's Hand

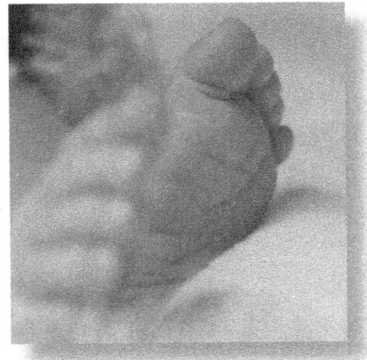

Ava's Feet

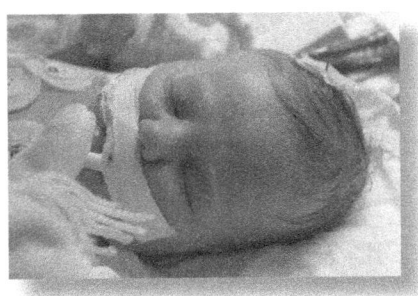

Ava

CHAPTER 30

Day 47

Dear Family and Friends,

My heart breaks as I write this last journal entry for Ava's CDH journey. My motivation to move forward comes from Ava, one breath at a time.

Yesterday around 1:00 p.m., Nancy and Ralph lifted Ava off her bed (while on ECMO) and put her in my arms. We sang our favorite songs and talked about our big plans for the future. Then Todd held her and promised her just about anything she wanted when we got home, even a pony. As she lay in my mom's arms, she opened her beautiful eyes and looked up at her grandma. My mom said she could feel how much Ava loved her as they gazed at each other. Ava listened to every word her Gaga said. All such precious memories.

Dr. Chen came over and said it was time to test clamping the ECMO cannulas. They put Ava back into my arms. I held her tight and prayed with her, "God, please be with Ava and give her strength to breathe on her own." As I rocked Ava and sang, "You Are My Sunshine," her cannulas were clamped. She fought hard but looked peaceful. As I held sweet Ava, Jesus wrapped His arms around her and took her to be with my grandmother, Janet Elaine, and my cousin Billy in heaven.

The doctors, surgeons, and nurses at Children's are so amazing. We could not have asked for anything more from them. We will forever be grateful for their care and compassion for Ava and our family.

Ava has impacted so many lives in her forty-seven days on earth. It's hard to find the words to express our gratitude to all of you who have loved, prayed, and hoped for our sweet Ava. We hope she finds a place in each of your hearts and brings you comfort in times of sorrow and joy in times of happiness.

With love and thanks,
Jennifer and Todd

Guestbook entries:

You don't know me, but I have been following Ava's journey. I wanted to let you know that I have been praying this whole time for this precious little one. I am without words after finding out about Ava this evening. I had my son right around the time Ava was born. I never knew what love like this is until he came into our lives. It has changed me forever. I know that Ava changed you forever as well and that you'll never be the same person again after she graced you with her life. I will continue to pray for you and Todd. I'm sending hugs your way and have a whole bunch of people praying too. You two have been through an incredible amount of pain, and I'm asking the Lord to send his strength and peace. May you be able to lean on him during this time.

"Come to me, all you who are weary and burdened, and I will give you rest." Matthew 11:28

Tamra Vandiver

~

Jennifer, Todd, and Karen, you are in my thoughts and prayers. Thanks for letting us be a part of Ava's beautiful life. Our prayers are with you.

Kelly Fedderm
Social Worker

~

Dear Jennifer and Todd,

My prayers have been for Ava and your family since the moment that Shawn and Stephanie shared your situation. I feel so honored to have gotten to meet Ava and to have been able to cheer for this precious little CDH fighter. There are really no words for the depth of my feelings right now; I could not fail to let you know how much we care. Last night, I was keeping the twins, and before Shawn got home, I was telling Kamryn that this was Ava's day to put on her boxing gloves and fight extra hard. All day I had prayed for her, but as the darkness came without word; my heart knew what my mind did not want to accept. I am so terribly sorry about your loss, and although we are not a part of your family, I know that all of our family shares your sadness in that we will not be granted the joy of seeing this little miracle grow up on earth. She *did* touch my life in her short time here; she *did* make a difference in the lives of so many. She was the most beautiful baby, and those gorgeous eyes spoke volumes about the love she received and gave in return. A part of her will always live in the hearts of those of us who shared her journey. May you know how much our family cares. She is a miracle and always will be, and now she is certainly an angelic one. Thank you for your precious daily updates and for allowing us into your private moments, especially in this last post. God bless you and your family now and in the days ahead. Know that sweet Ava will always be loved and remembered by our family and have a place in our hearts forever.

With love and heartfelt sympathy,

Ann Studdard and family

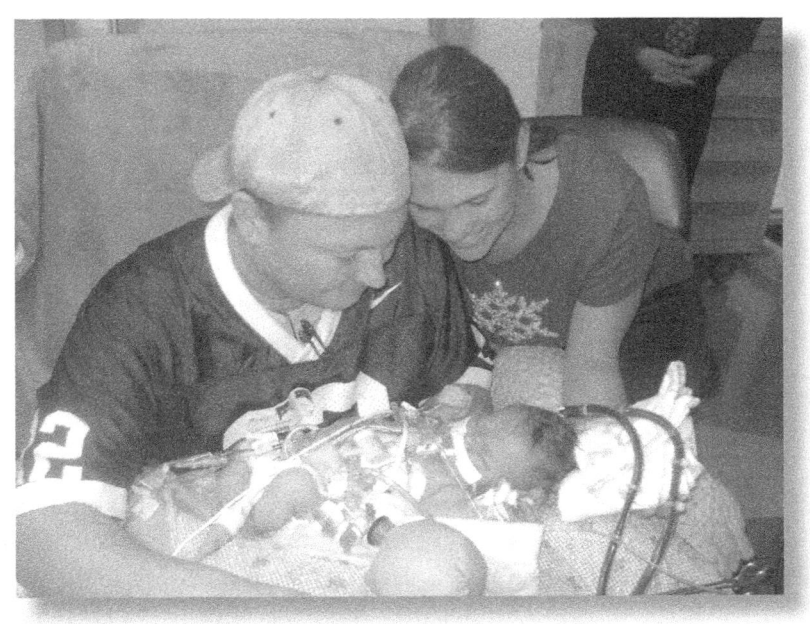

Family Picture

Daddy, Mommy and Ava

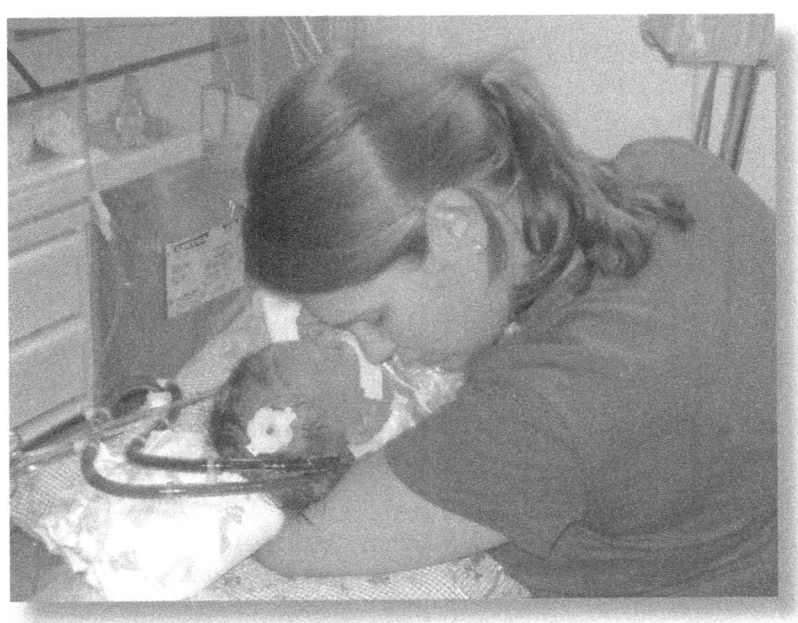

Praying with Ava

CHAPTER 31

A Brave Baby

Our sweet, courageous baby Ava Elaine earned her angel wings and is now resting peacefully in the arms of Christ. Her journey into this world began on October 22, 2010, in Dallas, Texas. Precious Ava's brave battle against congenital diaphragmatic hernia (CDH) ended on December 7, 2010, despite fighting with all of her amazing will and strength. She laced up her pink boxing gloves (from grandpa) to fight this condition, and along with the care and compassion of the brilliant staff at Children's Medical Center, she overcame many obstacles that CDH babies face. The doctors, surgeons, nurses, and ECMO team never gave up the battle against CDH, and neither did Ava. Her will to live and the dedication of her doctors led to breakthroughs in the treatment of CDH. We cannot be more thankful to the entire Children's family for all of the love and care they have shown. Ava stole the hearts of everyone who knew her or of her through reading her story.

Ava was preceded in death by her great-grandparents, Willis and Janet Elaine Rogy; Russel Rohde; James Robert and Sally Gardner; and her special cousin Billy Watt. Ava is survived by her loving parents, James Todd and Jennifer (Rohde) Dickerson; great grandmother Lorraine Rohde; adoring grandparents Jack and Karen Rohde; Ted and Angeline DeMoss, big brother Jason Dickerson, Aunt Kristi (Bryan) Hunter, and Aunt Darby Dickerson. Ava has two special cousins, Mandy and Ally Hunter, who showered her with loving notes and pictures that decorated her room. Jason, Mandy, and Ally are saddened that they never had the chance to play with Ava. Ava is also survived by great-aunts and -uncles: Barb (Rob) Kelsh, Lori (Dave) Morse, Bill (Becky) Rogy, Tom (Debbie) Rohde, Debby Rohde, Eric (Michele) Rohde, and a host of loving cousins and dear friends.

A memorial service to celebrate and honor Ava's life will be held on Tuesday, December 14, 2:00 p.m., at First Presbyterian Church, 408 Park Avenue, Dallas, Texas 75201. Visitation will be held on Monday, December 13, from 6:30 p.m. to 8:30 p.m. at Restland Funeral Home, 13005 Greenville Ave, Dallas, Texas 75243.

In lieu of flowers, the family requests that donations be made in honor of Ava Elaine Dickerson to First Presbyterian Developmental Day School, 408 Park Avenue, Dallas, Texas 75201. First Presbyterian is currently under construction. The church is expanding its welcome center and historic facilities, rejuvenating its youth area, and creating a beautiful chapel garden. It will be through donations that a memorial monument, such as a bench or fountain, is made in Ava's name. It will serve as a place for prayer, reflection, and healing to all.

Special thanks to all of Ava's prayer warriors, including family and friends, many of whom we have never met, who gave us support and hope every day of Ava's life.

Sweet Ava, as you danced in the light with joy, love lifted you. As you brushed against this world so gently, you lifted us.

We will miss and love you every day for the rest of our lives, until we meet again, our sweet, precious baby Ava.

CHAPTER 32

Make Every Day Count

At Ava's visitation last night, I met a new friend, Kelsey. She's a friend of my cousin Kim and has followed Ava's journey with us. She was so moved and inspired by Ava's short life here that she got a tattoo on her ankle—47 Days—a reminder that each and every day in our lives is important. Kelsey, thank you for sharing and being there last night. Hugs to you; you are so sweet.

I have another make-every-day-count story to share about Ava's forty-seven days. Please read the e-mail from my dear friend Wendel. His son, Tyler, sums it up best. Thanks for sharing, Wendel; hugs to your beautiful family.

Wendel and Tyler's words:

> Ava touched so many lives; you will never know. It was ironic to read the last journal entry about the tattoo. The kids have been following along with Ava and were saddened to hear of her passing. Forty-seven days just doesn't seem fair. Then Tyler said, "Now my number has meaning."

When we got home from Ava's visitation, I received a phone call from Tiffany, Sterling's grandmother. Sterling suffered cardiac arrest earlier that day and joined Ava in heaven. I was speechless. I did not think this day could be filled with any more sadness. The night we left the hospital I gave Sterling Ava's silver tinsel Christmas tree. Ava loved looking at the lights sparkle as I told her Christmas stories.

I thought Ava would want her fellow fighter next door to have it. Sterling was doing so well and scheduled to come off ECMO in a few days. The news was unexpected, and I felt so sad for Sterling's mom, Patrice, that she too would be spending Christmas without her baby. Another reminder, though very sad, that we should make every day count.

Well, it's time for me to get ready for Ava's funeral. Oh, this hurts so very much, and I'm so thankful to have my family here to lean on. Thanks to everyone for your outpouring of support, prayers, and love the last few days. To my sisters: AOE.

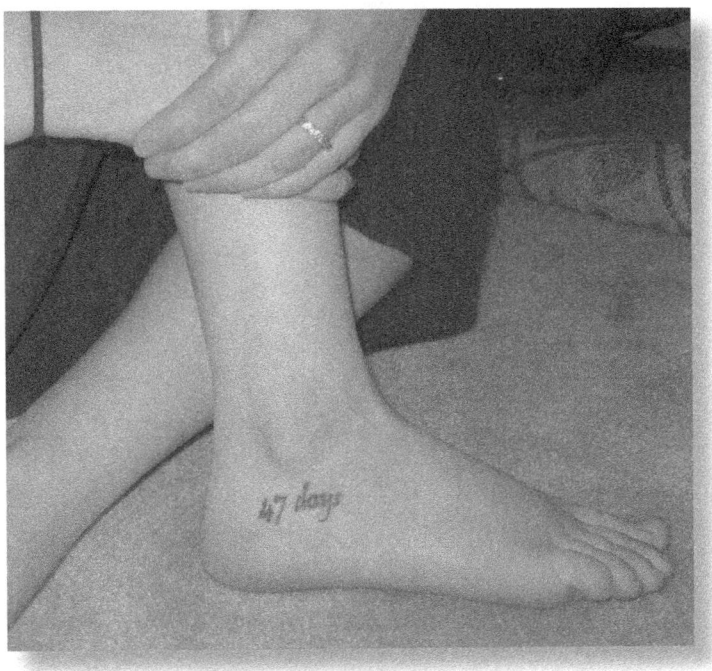

Kelsey's tattoo

Tyler Werland

CHAPTER 33

Beautiful Words

Ava's visitation and memorial service were beautiful. She touched so many lives and brought family, friends, and otherwise strangers together through her valiant fight for life. It is so painful for me, as her mommy, to understand why God did not allow her to stay here with us and continue her impact. I pray for my heart to heal in knowing that her impact in heaven is just as glorious.

I thought I would share some of the words spoken at Ava's memorial during this week leading up to Christmas. Reading them helps me heal and remember this is a wonderful time of the year.

I had asked Dr. Thomas to provide a few words for Ava's memorial video in which he so kindly responded and my mom so eloquently read:

> Medicine often answers the "what" and "how" questions. It can never answer the "why" questions, those questions that linger unanswered even when we know what happened and how.
>
> *Why* did Ava touch us in a way that other children haven't. *Why* did she make us care more than we thought possible before meeting her? *Why* did she come to us, affect us so deeply, and then leave?
>
> Though medical training does not prepare one to answer these questions, I have pondered them every day since meeting Ava and her family, and some early answers have begun to emerge.

Ava was endowed with a unique grace that those who knew her could feel. Perhaps she was a vehicle for a greater force or maybe she possessed a larger-than-life charisma. Ava made me want to be a better doctor, to push beyond the limits of my usual practice, to find new solutions to intractable problems. She made me want to make others care deeply for her, too. She brought a team closer together than ever in our experience at Children's. Surgeons, pediatricians, ECMO specialists, nurses, and respiratory therapists worked hand in glove to try to save Ava. She was the center of our universe; we, mere planets with a skill or two.

If her presence engendered all this goodness, then, *why* did she have to leave? That's the toughest question of them all.

Perhaps she knew she would wear all of us out if she kept pushing us the way she did (though I'm certain we all would have kept going until we simply dropped).

Perhaps she was a seed planted in all of us that is now growing inside, making us better caregivers, better spouses, better parents, and better children. And each time we reach out to help ease someone else's pain, we will see Ava and push ourselves to give more than we thought possible.

Thank you, sweet Ava.

CHAPTER 34

※

Reflection for Ava Elaine Dickerson

By Elias Lopez, Chaplain
Children's Medical Center

What can we say about the life of Ava Elaine Dickerson? We could say that it was too short, but this fails to do justice to the significance of her time with us. Ava was truly unique. She was one of a kind. The medical staff quickly learned Ava's name, and her beauty became legendary. During one of the first psychosocial rounds, we referred to her as "the little cutie."

She was loved so much by her parents and grandparents. They were constantly at her side, talking with her, singing to her, playing soothing music for her, and caring for her in every way one could think of. They taught me that one never gets bored when it comes to waiting with one's child.

I remember our time together when Ava first arrived at Children's and all we could ask was why. Why did this happen? Why do bad things happen to good people? And specifically, why was this happening to Ava? We struggled with these questions for a good while, and probably even now we still wonder some of the same things. I wish I had the answer, I wish I could explain suffering and why Ava died, but even if I could, I'm not sure that it would take away our pain. That we feel this pain reflects something about the gift that Ava was in our lives. It also reflects that great love we all had for this special child.

Ava quickly got a reputation for being a fighter. From the time she spent in the NICU, Ava clenched her fists in preparation for her fight. Grandpa bought her a set of pink boxing gloves, and Team Ava was always standing at the ready in her corner. The staff at the hospital marveled at her ability to overcome a number of obstacles and difficult medical procedures. She would surprise us all, by telling us in her own way that she was not giving up without a fight.

I was fortunate to witness many tender moments between Ava and Jennifer. They would sit together taking pleasure in each other's company for hours. That special bond between mother and child united them in a way that seemed to melt away their surroundings, and nothing could interrupt their moment. Ava enjoyed spending time with her parents and grandmother. She would open her eyes, raise her arms, and wiggle her toes; she was letting them know it was time for a story, it was time to play. And no one could ever turn down a request from Ava.

I remember stopping by her room to visit with Ava. Karen was there, and after sharing for a little bit, we decided to pray. All three of us held hands, Karen, Ava and I; and as we prayed, Ava squeezed my finger so tight. I felt her praying for me. That was Ava, giving us as much as we wanted to give her. Karen shared a drawing with me from one of her family members that captured the sun breaking through the clouds. This image was very helpful in reminding us that Ava was shining through in the midst of her aliment and all the medical jargon and equipment. She illuminated beyond her room, beyond the hospital, into the hearts and minds of all her supporters. Her room was adorned with all the expressions of love that were sent to her, and her heart was warmed by all of you. Everyone who walked into her room could feel the love and support that surrounded her and her parents.

I know that we can all say that we have learned a lot from this young child; that our lives will never be the same because she touched each of us in a special way. I learned that physical stature does not determine the size of one's spirit; that while you may be small, a big spirit is what you need for the fight. I learned that the most important moments in life are those spent in the company of the ones you love; that our relationships bring meaning to our lives. I learned that communication is not restricted to words; that we can invite people, and God, into a relationship through our personality. I learned that we bless others as we are being blessed ourselves; that we can give while we receive. Ava demonstrated that in her life, she was full of life. While we say good-bye to Ava today, we also say hello to the love that is the meaning of her life. We all have memories of Ava, and today we will try to strengthen those memories and say hello to the Ava, who lives on within us in our hearts and minds.

Let us remember Ava, this little fighter, this "little cutie," who kept us all wondering, waiting, learning, and loving.

Amen.

Chapter 35

━━━ ⚬⚬⚬ ━━━

Christmas Eve

Merry Christmas, Happy Holidays, Everyone,

I'm sitting here at my mom and dad's by the fire, wishing Ava were here. We decorated cookies earlier today. My twin nieces, Mandy and Ally, made two for Ava: one in the shape of an angel with pink wings and red hair and one in the shape of a star with her name. My mom and I take them shopping every Christmas so they can buy each other a gift. Mandy and I were at Justice (anyone with a preteen girl knows this store), and the song "Hallelujah" came on through the store's speakers. I immediately teared up, froze, and felt like the world around me stopped. Mandy came over, wrapped her arms around me, and said, "Aunt Jenny, this is one the songs from Ava's video." I've always said those are my two angels sent from heaven, and they are the sweetest girls!

My aunt Lori lights a candle every Christmas for her son, Billy, and her granddaughter, Hannah, in their honor. She suggested we light one tomorrow for Ava at 6:00 p.m. CST. I hope you can join us in lighting a candle so that the world will sparkle as we remember sweet Ava and to make every day in our lives count.

I'd like to share with you my aunt Lori's words that she spoke at Ava's funeral:

> I want to start by saying to Jennifer, Todd, Grandma
> Karen and Grandpa Jack that there are no words that can

describe what you are going through. I feel your pain, and my heart breaks for you. No one can claim to have the reasons as to why, but there are things that I know for certain. Jennifer, you were an amazing little girl who has grown up to be an amazing woman. Anyone who knows you knew that you would be the most wonderful of mothers. There is a mother here who also holds that rank of most wonderful: Ava's grandma, your mom, my sister Karen. Having said that, it was no surprise to any of us when you gave birth to amazing Ava!

There is more that I know for certain because I was privileged enough to witness the love among all of you and Ava. Ava fought a hard fight for you as well as for herself because of that love. I know for certain that not once was Ava ever alone during those precious forty-seven days. I could feel the love that you shared with her.

I know for certain that Ava helped many people: family, friends, and people who you don't know and may never know, just by being Ava. How could any of us not be changed by knowing this little champion? We would all be lucky to have half of the guts and determination that Ava had when facing challenges in our own lives.

I know for certain that Ava is as proud to be your daughter, as you are to be her mommy and daddy. Ava was an angel on earth and is now flying high with the angels in heaven.

I know for certain that Ava will be there in your heart and on your mind for every minute of every day for the rest of your lives.

From all of your family, Ava, you've inspired us. We love you. We miss you. Fly high among the clouds, and we will meet again!

Love you,
Great-Aunt Lori

Jennifer Rohde Dickerson

I would be honored if you would light a candle tomorrow for Ava. Remember and cherish tomorrow's ultimate meaning. Hug your kiddos tight.

Love and peace,
Jennifer

Chapter 36

Aunt Bec

The prayers, support, and acts of kindness we have received have been overwhelming and are helping us through this most difficult time in our lives. I continue to hang on to every memory we created with Ava in those forty-seven precious days. Reading Ava's journal and guestbook over and over helps my broken heart heal. Thank you to everyone who has taken the time in writing and reading here.

I would like to share the words that my aunt Becky spoke at Ava's funeral:

> I will never forget the day that I got the call from Karen telling me that something could be wrong with little baby Ava. My heart dropped, and so did I, straight to my knees to pray for her. As we all now know, the news was not good and our baby Ava was going to have a fight at birth. After talking to the family, we decided that I would come down to Dallas for her birth. In my mind, I was thinking that I would be coming down to help out in any way I could. I could pick the twins up from school, take care of the dogs, and make sure there would be something to eat when needed. No problem, I could handle that, but what I didn't expect was the life-changing event that I was about to experience.
>
> Ava Elaine arrived in this world surrounded by love and prayers. When she was less than twenty-four hours old, I had the privilege of meeting her. She was hooked up to

too many machines for one little girl, but the funny thing was I never really noticed them. What I saw was the most beautiful little red-headed baby I have ever seen. She was magical and at first sight had captured my heart. I was in love, and there was no turning back from the journey that was to be Ava's. Every waking moment I could think of nothing else. I even dreamed of her often at night.

I have been a born-again Christian for many years, but never before had I sensed the Lord's presence as I did during Ava's struggle. I witnessed miracles that at times I felt foolish to even imagine possible. The first one that I remember was when she developed a blood clot and, instead of dissolving, it was breaking up into little clots which were going to her legs. She lost the pulse in her tiny foot and the doctors said there was nothing more they could do. I felt helpless, and all I could think to do was pray. So down on my knees I went right in the hallway of the Children's hospital. I can't recall how long it was, but I know it was within a couple of hours that we heard that the pulse was back and the clots were gone! Whenever I was in the room with Ava, I felt a closeness to God that I'd never imagined possible, and for that I have Ava to thank. There were other miracles, and I could go on and on about the amazing ways in which Ava impacted my life and the life of many others, but I am sure that by now you get the idea.

In the end, we did not have the answers to the prayers that we had hoped for, but we still had answers. My faith tells me that Ava is in heaven, dancing with the angels, happy and whole. She is without machines, free of pain, and surrounded by Christ's love. I also know that although it will never be long enough, Jennifer and Todd were given time to let Ava know how loved and cherished she was. She recognized her mommy's voice and calmed at her touch. She listened to Grandma as she talked to her and told her how much she was cherished. Many times in our life, forty-seven days can past quickly and without any real significant meaning, but to our sweet baby Ava, Jennifer, Todd, Karen, and everyone else who loved her, it was a lifetime of love that will be with us always. My prayers will continue to go up, asking for healing, comfort, and peace to those whose lives Ava touched. I love you, Ava, and know that I will see you again. The things of this life pass in a flash, but our eternal life with Jesus will last forever.

CHAPTER 37

———— ∞∞∞ ————

New Year's Day

Reflecting back on 2010, it was set up to be a promising year filled with happiness and new beginnings. Todd and I took a wonderful trip to Mexico with my parents in January. We found out in February, I was pregnant. We bought a new home in a perfect neighborhood filled with young children for Jason (my stepson) and "Baby D" (at the time) to play and grow up with. We spent a week at Lake Norfork at our annual family reunion and created many special memories. Todd's restaurant, Angry Dog, celebrated its twentieth anniversary. We celebrated my parents' forty-fourth wedding anniversary over a great weekend with family and friends. I experienced and was blessed with the miracle of pregnancy and childbirth.

2010 was the happiest year of my life, yet on this first day of 2011, I feel completely empty.

Our pastor told Todd and me that we would grieve in our own ways. People have told us it will get better with time. We have good days, bad days, and better days. I know with the love of my husband, my parents, my family, and my friends I will make it through each day. I know with my faith I will make it through this life until I get to hold Ava again.

I do know Ava is an angel in heaven protecting us. A twelve-foot beam with a chandelier fell in the foyer of my parents' house yesterday, in the entry way where we all enter their home, where their dog laid the day before for hours while my mom cleaned her floors, where my aunts and uncles were sitting at my birthday dinner a few weeks ago. My mom sat in her chair, reading, and thought of getting the paper moments before the beam crashed down. Thankfully, no one was hurt. I can think of only two words to describe it: *divine intervention.*

Thank you, sweet Ava.

I miss you so much it hurts through every part of my body. We spent most of 2010 inseparable. I know in 2011 you will never be separate from my thoughts and never be separate from my heart.

I pray the New Year brings all of you joy, peace, and happiness.

CHAPTER 38

One Day at a Time

One month ago I held our precious sweet Ava in my arms for the first time *and the last time.*

I have spent many days and sleepless nights since December 7, recollecting those last twenty-four hours we had with Ava. I could tell you minute by minute what happened. I struggled as the social worker came into Ava's room and told me about a photographer who volunteered with a group called Now I Lay Me Down to Sleep. Why was she suggesting that I take Ava's last pictures? Todd and I called a few friends to come meet Ava, and our family that was in town came to see her, too. I took pictures and a video of my sister, Kristi, with Ava. But all this extra attention was just to wish her well as she was coming off ECMO the next day, *right?*

My mom, Todd, and I woke up in Ava's room, as we had all forty-seven days before, to the doctor's rounds at 9:00 a.m. to recap and review the day's plan. *Her chest x-ray looks better than yesterday; she required less medication overnight; she's peeing on her own!* Ava was telling us she's ready to come off ECMO. Our favorite nurse, Nancy, was there that day, even though she worked only Sundays and Mondays. That's how the staff works at Children's. They are genuine, amazing, wonderful people. Nancy came in on Tuesday, after two days of twelve-hour shifts with Ava, to make sure everything was ready for her big day.

We never gave up hope. We prayed for a miracle. *Just one last miracle, God, please, please, please. Let her breathe; let her lungs open; let her heart pump her own blood through her precious body.*

When I look back at the pictures from the day I got to hold Ava for the first time, I see my smile as big and happy as it's ever been. So I remind myself that it was a great day. God did answer my prayers. Ava *was* breathing on her own; her lungs *were* open, *but so are her wings.*

I have had some pretty gut-wrenching days since December 7, but it seems like God is putting people and their actions in place to make sure I keep going. The weekend following Ava's funeral, I decided to try and have a "normal" Saturday with my stepson, Jason. We went to my office and ate breakfast together while I did a little work. *OK, that was easy enough, now let's try Target since I had not been to a grocery store in weeks.* As we walked in hand in hand, there were moms and their babies in strollers and carriers all around us. *Inhale-exhale-inhale-exhale.* Fighting back tears, I put Jason in a cart, and a sweet voice called my name. I turned around to see Li Ern (Dr. Chen) coming toward us. "This must be Jason. Hi, nice to meet you!" Then she told me she went to the symphony a few days before and listened to a beautiful voice that sounded like an angel. She looked her name up in the program, and it was Ava. We hugged, and I thanked her for sharing the heartwarming story and told her that she turned my sad moment happy. On Christmas Eve, before driving to my parents' house, I got the mail. I went for the biggest envelope first; it was from the funeral home. Having better intuition, Todd tried to stop me. But before he could, I pulled out Ava's death certificate. *How cruel and unfair that I receive my baby's death certificate before her birth certificate!* The next letter I opened was a card with a return address from Courtney Mahr, one of my Alpha Phi pledge sisters, whom I had not seen or talked to since graduation. She got together twenty-five of my sisters and made a donation to Ava's memorial fund. The words she wrote were so sweet and made my heart smile. *What a generous act of kindness from my sisters and a reminder of how special they are to me.*

CHAPTER 39

Faith, Hope, and Love

I knew when I walked out of room 12-263 at Children's, my home for forty-seven days, that a part of me would never be the same. I begged Todd to let me stay just one more night on my couch. My family started taking down and packing up her things: her pink boxing gloves, drawings from the twins, an angel of hope from Howard and Silvia, pictures from the day she was born, her cross necklace from Jani, her books, and her blankets. I turned to my Dad and asked him to tell everyone to please stop. *Wait, please wait, I'm sleeping here tonight. Please, let me stay with Ava.*

Nancy promised to take care of her and convinced me it was best to go home. As I walked out with a broken heart, I realized all Ava had ever known was love.

Today was the first day back to Children's. Mom and I took lunch to the twelfth floor. Precious Kelly met us downstairs and told us she was proud of us for being brave and coming back. I think it's part of the healing process for us. As we rode up the elevator, my heart was riding up my throat. My eyes were blurred with tears as she swiped her card and opened the doors to Ava's hall. We walked in and stood still; the smell brought back many emotions; my knees were weak and I was starting to think this may be too soon. At that moment, Ralph and his smile came around the corner to embrace us. *Whew, thank you, God, and thank you, Ava.* It was so nice to see Ava's nurses, respiratory therapists, ECMO specialists, and doctors. We wanted to say *thank you* to the people who cared for Ava. Their tremendous skill and talent, combined with their caring manner, is a credit to the medical profession. It was a good visit, and I'll be praying for my knees to stay strong tonight when we go back for the night shift.

One month ago, Todd and I stood together at Ava's funeral as I read a letter I wrote earlier that day:

Dear Sweet Ava,

Aunt Lori told me it helped her in the healing process to write letters to Billy. I know you are with Billy right now.

Today I want to tell you some of the things I miss and will miss so dearly about you. I never got to hear the sound of your voice, even though I am sure it is sweet. I will miss your first words, the first time you sit up, the first time you crawl, and your first steps. I will miss rocking you to sleep and taking long walks in your stroller by the lake. I will miss birthday parties and play dates. I will miss watching you grow into a beautiful young woman, Ava. I will miss watching you play sports, dance, and learn at school. I will miss you at our family reunion every year. I will miss taking you to New York City with all the girls to watch Broadway shows and shop until Grandpa calls and tells us to stop. I know you would have made such an impact in your life here—look what you did in forty-seven days! I will miss knowing and seeing that. We had big plans, and not a second goes by in my day that I don't think about you and wish you were here.

I will miss watching your big brother, Jason, play with you. He's a little young now to understand, but once he gets older, he will know all about you. I will miss your cousins Mandy and Ally, teaching you everything they know (and that's a lot). I know Aunt Kristi and Uncle Bryan hug their girls tighter now because of you.

I will miss watching Grandma care, hold, and love you. She's such an amazing mom, Ava, and I was going to try and be just like her with you.

I will miss watching Grandpa teach you how to grip and swing a golf club. I would have been right next to you as he told you the same things he always told me: "You're dipping your shoulder again, Ava. Keep your head down." Mandy and Ally are learning to play golf, too. I know we would have had so much fun golfing together.

I could tell you were going to be a daddy's girl, like me, Ava. I am going to have to write a separate letter about Daddy, okay? But let me tell you, he loves me and Jason more than anything, and he was really looking forward to showing you that same love. But now you're in his heart forever.

Today's a big day for us, Ava. I am going to have to say good-bye to your sweet presence in a few hours. But then you will always be with us. And your sweet spirit will always be in our hearts. I know you are a precious angel now, looking over us and protecting us.

Fly high and breathe easy, sweet Ava. I love you more than I can ever say.

Big Brother, Jason

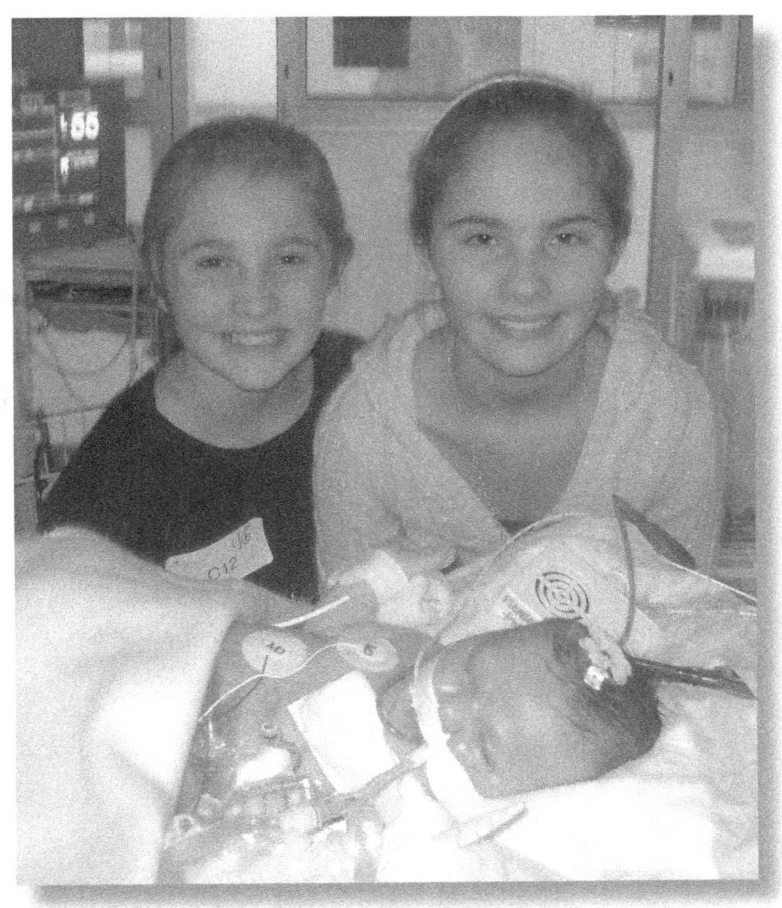

The Granddaughters: Mandy, Ally and Ava

CHAPTER 40

———— ∞∞∞ ————

Watching for Angels

I am picking up Jason from school as Todd's Achilles tendon is still healing from surgery. One day as we walked out of the building toward the west, he said, "Mamma Nenny, look at that pretty sunset." I said, "Yes, Jason, it's beautiful. What colors do you see?" He chose just one color, one word (which is not like him): "*Pink.*" So I told him his little sister in heaven makes the sunsets pink. He replied, "Why?" I told him that is Ava's favorite color. As we kept walking hand in hand, his head was still looking up and around at the sky. I asked him what he was doing, and he told me he was waiting to see Ava fly by. *We can learn so much from our children. Keep life simple, embrace God's beauty, and watch for angels.*

From my aunt Lori:
Ava's red sunshine

It was the end of November. Ava's lung was filling up with blood and collapsing, and we all were worried that this might be it. If her one good lung was not working, we were going to lose her for sure. From the time our sweet Ava had come into this world, October 22, we had prayed many prayers, but this day in November, I asked God, "Please give me some kind of sign that our girl is going to be okay. Please God, anything that we can hold on to at this time." I prayed and prayed all day. That day was cloudy with no sign of sun. I looked toward the sky and asked God again to provide a sign, and as I was looking at the sky, just as I asked again, the most beautiful red sun appeared. I had never seen anything like this in my life, and I'm fifty-seven years old. I could not believe my eyes. I couldn't wait to call my sister Karen and let her know that Ava's lung was going to get better. I asked Karen to call Jennifer and to tell her what I saw. As it turned out, Ava did improve, and she amazed us once again. With God's help, she made it through another difficult time. Ava continued to fight the good fight until the evening of December 7, 2010. When you lose a child, what you want the most is to have them back, which you know is impossible. The next thing you want is just to know that they are okay. Sometimes you have to wait a while for that sign to come. On the morning of August 10, 2011, I got that sign. I walked out to get my newspaper and was greeted by the most beautiful red sun. This made the second time in my life now seeing this red sun, and I knew it was from Ava saying, "Good morning, don't worry. I'm doing fine."

From my mom, Karen:

My family is amazing. During Ava's CDH journey, we were never alone. The week before Ava's birth, my sister-in-law, Becky, came to stay with us. When she needed to get back home, my sister Lori and her husband, Dave, came for the next two weeks. Next came my sister Barb and her husband, Rob. They cooked; cleaned; took food to the hospital; took care of Jack, Maggie (our dog), and the two cats; and picked up the twins from school. Our home was a whirlwind of activity!

After Ava's funeral, we gave our thanks to and said our good-byes to all the relatives who had been here since before day one of Ava's incredible journey. I found myself alone and lonely in our living room, sitting by the fire. I was missing Ava after spending every day and many nights in her sweet presence. I closed my eyes and prayed that God might show me a sign that He was watching over her and loving her as we had. After several minutes, I felt a hand on my shoulder. I opened my eyes and looked up, but there was no one there. *Or was there?* I knew then that our sweet Ava was well and safe in His arms.

In the fall of 2011, my mom, Ally, Mandy, Jason, and I spent an afternoon at the Dallas Arboretum. It's always hard to be somewhere with a lot of other families and strollers, but we all embraced the sunny day with smiles while walking through beautiful flowers and pumpkin patches. Many toddlers were dressed in their Halloween costumes, and parents were snapping pictures everywhere. During times like these, it's hard not to think of what I would be doing if Ava were here. I'm sure she'd be dressed as something super-cute like a ladybug. I'm sure Mandy, Ally, and Jason would be taking turns of who gets to pull the wagon next while Ava rides and laughs along. We stopped to eat lunch at the outside café. I got the kids settled at a table while my mom ordered at the counter. She came back with drinks and napkins, and I told her I would go wait for the food. I noticed they were calling order numbers, and I turned around and asked my mom what number we were. She replied, "Our favorite number," and handed me a ticket with the number 47 printed on it.

We both smiled and I knew sweet Ava was there, spending the day with us. I accepted I could not take a picture of her nestled in a pumpkin patch but knew I had my angel watching over us.

Ava's heavenly birthday was approaching the first week of December 2011. Our church held a "Blue Christmas" service the Sunday before. It was a service of grief and healing during a time of year that hurts the most as we miss loved ones. I asked Todd to go with my mom and me, hoping it could help ease our anxious feelings for the week to come. Our pastor, Joe Clifford, gave us the best advice after Ava's memorial service, telling Todd and me that everyone grieves in their own way: "Understand that you two may grieve differently, and respect, love, and be there for each other as you go through each day." I knew it would be hard for Todd to enter into the chapel where we had Ava's memorial service. I knew he would look at the table that says In Remembrance of Me, and think that's where Ava laid in her tiny casket. The service was beautiful and peaceful. We wrote notes on ornaments and, as the congregation sang, we placed them on a tree and held the sweet memories of Ava close in our hearts. As we returned to the pew, I noticed the last song on the list was hymn 47. The organist started playing, and my heart smiled as I opened the hymnal to 47: *Still, Still, Still.* It is a beautiful Christmas song, also known as a lullaby, which describes the peace of the infant Jesus and His mother as they sleep.

I knew Ava, our angel, was right there in the chapel with us. I knew she was lifting her daddy's heart up to God to help heal it back together.

CHAPTER 41

Expectations and Reality

Ava is three months old today. I'm sure we would have been at the photographer this week taking precious pictures. I realize I have to face reality, which invites sorrow back into my heart.

Sometimes I face life with the following formula: Expectations minus reality equals disappointment. Todd and I were so excited after my positive pregnancy test. I continued to check the test for an hour just to make sure it did not change, guarding my expectations. When the call came from the doctor that afternoon, confirming my blood test that we were indeed pregnant, I fell in love with our baby. I was *completely* in love. After the twelve-week mark, and as I made my way into the second trimester, I started planning and creating expectations for our future.

One of my expectations was to get back to work before Ava started day school. I had a bassinet ready, a bouncy chair for my office, and a cooler for bottles to take my milk so everyone could feed her. I expected to go back to work full-time after the holidays. So when I got in my car on January third to head to my office, I faced reality and felt the pain of disappointment. *Will this enormous gap between my expectations and reality ever close?* I started driving, called my mom, and kept going past my exit. Twenty minutes later I was pulling into my parents' driveway. I just could not face reality that day. I am thankful that my work family took care of our customers and my administrative responsibilities through this difficult time in my life. I am truly blessed for having their love and support.

Another reality check was the day I donated my frozen milk for sick infants. Sure, I am glad to help other babies, but those were not my expectations as I pumped every day. I counted the bags as I filled the coolers. I could have fed Ava over a hundred times, and the reality of never feeding her summoned grief.

One thing I do know and can expect every single day is for Todd to love me. He promised to hold me every night when I told him how empty my arms felt. I get through my days knowing I'll be in his arms at night.

As I face the reality of life, every day I give thanks to God for giving us Ava. I find comfort in my faith, my hope for the future, and my prayers. Many thanks to everyone for your love, prayers, and support! Todd, my parents and family, and my friends, I know, will help fill that gap between my expectations and reality.

CHAPTER 42

— ◦⊗◦ —

It Is Well with My Soul

As I drove to church this morning, I thanked God for many blessings this past week. My dad had a successful hip replacement surgery and is at home recovering. Work is good, and I am getting back to a normal schedule. Todd's Achilles tendon is healing, and he is becoming more mobile! As always, I thanked God for Ava and then reflected on how she's changed my life.

Tomorrow would have been Ava's first day at school. I remember receiving the letter and proudly hanging it on the refrigerator next to her sonogram picture: "Todd and Jennifer: The day school is pleased to inform you that we can officially confirm space availability for Ava starting February 1, 2011, in Infant 1 with Ms. Marvetta and Ms. Marta." I thought, *The first of many acceptance letters for Ava!* The truth is that if I were to drive Ava to school tomorrow, I would not have driven to church today. Ava has strengthened many relationships in my life, but the one that she has impacted most is the relationship I have with God. I find comfort and peace in Scripture: "And the peace of God, which transcends all understanding, will guard your hearts and your minds in Christ Jesus" (Philippians 4:7 New International Version). "He heals the brokenhearted and binds up their wounds" (Psalm 147:3 New International Version). God is healing my broken heart, and I have Him to thank for Ava and Ava to thank for my relationship with Him. My heart smiles as I type the numbers 4 and 7 several times together when referencing scripture. Coincidence? *I think not.*

Todd and I went to dinner Friday night. It was the first time since Ava was born that my hair did not automatically go into a ponytail.

It was the first time I was confident about wearing mascara, hoping it would not be captured with tears and run down my face. It was the first time I took a few minutes to pick out clothes (and shoes). My heart is healing. *My heart is healing one day at a time, with Todd holding my hand, and God and His Son in my heart.*

A good family friend, Robert Little, sang a hymn at Ava's services: "It Is Well With My Soul." *Robert* shared the story behind the hymn, and I remember reading the e-mail one night with Todd as we planned Ava's memorial service. It's a tragic but beautiful story—pain and peace all together, which is exactly how I feel. Thank you, Robert, for choosing the perfect song for Ava. It *is* well with my soul. Following is the story:

> Horatio Spafford (1828-1888) was a wealthy Chicago lawyer with a thriving legal practice, a beautiful home, a wife, four daughters, and a son. He was also a devout Christian and faithful student of the Scriptures. His circle of friends included Dwight L. Moody, Ira Sankey, and various other well-known Christians of the day.
>
> At the very height of his financial and professional success, Horatio and his wife Anna suffered the tragic loss of their young son. Shortly thereafter on October 8, 1871, the Great Chicago Fire destroyed almost every real estate investment that Spafford had.
>
> In 1873, Spafford scheduled a boat trip to Europe in order to give his wife and daughters a much-needed vacation and time to recover from the tragedy. He also went to join Moody and Sankey on an evangelistic campaign in England. Spafford sent his wife and daughters ahead of him while he remained in Chicago to take care of some unexpected last minute business. Several days later he received notice that his family's ship had encountered a collision. All four of his daughters drowned; only his wife had survived.
>
> With a heavy heart, Spafford boarded a boat that would take him to his grieving Anna in England. It was on this trip

that he penned those now famous words, "When sorrow like sea billows roll; it is well, it is well with my soul."

Philip Bliss (1838-1876), composer of many songs, including "Hold the Fort," "Let the Lower Lights Be Burning," and "Jesus Loves Even Me," was so impressed with Spafford's life and the words of his hymn that he composed a beautiful piece of music to accompany the lyrics. The song was published by Bliss and Sankey in 1876.

My hope is that if you are hurting or face struggles or challenges in your life, Ava's journey may inspire you to turn to God for resolve and peace.

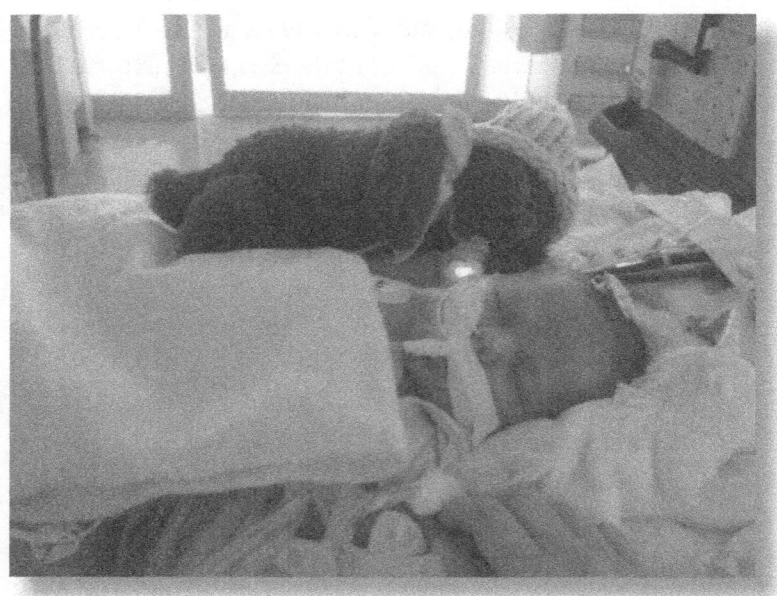

Baylor and Ava

Ava's first Teddy Bear, Baylor, was given to her by Robert Little during a visit to the hospital. Baylor's hat was hand-made by Dr. Thomas's daughter. It was a gift for Ava and given to her after our first few days at Children's.

CHAPTER 43

A Letter to Ava

Dear Sweet Ava,

I pray to God every day that He tells you how much we love and miss you. I pray that He and Jesus hold you close and let you watch over us. I imagine you with soft red hair and big beautiful wings. I dream of you often and have faith that you are happy and healthy. I wake your daddy up in the middle of the night so he will hold me tight and fill my empty arms. Do you hear me when I read to you in your nursery, Ava? Was that you who put the bag of your blankets and washcloths from the hospital in the clothes hamper? Were you telling me that it's okay for me to wash them now? I have so many special people in my life because of you, Ava. I thank God for them, too.

Today we went to a service at the funeral home to honor you. As we walked in, I asked your grandma, "Was this the same chapel where we had Ava's visitation service?" I did not recognize it without the pictures, stuffed animals, and mementos of you. It seemed so much smaller than when we were there in December. I think it was because your tiny casket made the chapel seem enormous. The pastor's message was simple and heartfelt: "Today we gather to remember a loved one. It could be a mother, father, grandparent, sister, brother, or even the tragic loss of a son or *daughter*." The pastor said a familiar quote by Emily Dickinson that reminds me of you:

"Hope is the thing with feathers
That perches in the soul
And sings the tune without the words
And never stops at all."

As the pastor read your name aloud, "Ava Elaine Dickerson," we stood, and a candle was lit in your memory. Your two special cousins, Ally and Mandy, sat on either side of me. They miss you very much. Your picture is in their locker at school, they proudly wear their CDH Awareness wrist bands, and they write the number 47 just about any time they have a pen or marker in their hands! At the end of the service, we went outside for a dove release. We stood in a circle, and they played a song that we put on your memorial video. It's called "Fly" and it's the perfect song for you, sweet Ava. As soon as the music came on, my heart smiled and tears streamed down my face. As they released the doves, I thought of your sweet spirit leaving us for heaven as I held you in my arms. When we got in the car, I shared the beautiful picture captured of the doves dancing around us. *Is that you, Ava, flying high and breathing easy?*

Ava, so many of our family and friends hold their children closer because of you. It's one of the so many because-of-Ava reasons I have written down in my pink journal. When I am sad or having a not-so-great day, I can open that journal and read of the things that you did in your forty-seven days here with us. I reflect on your strength, courage, and fighting spirit and realize *I will make it today, and then I thank God for you.*

Good night, sweet Ava. I love you. Mommy.

Ava's Dove

A peaceful dove taking flight reminding us of Ava
flying high and breathing easy in heaven.

CHAPTER 44

———∞∞∞———

CDH Awareness

Dear Family and Friends,

I wanted to let everyone know today is CDH Awareness Day! April 19, 2010, marks the first-year anniversary that the trademark was removed from "Congenital Diaphragmatic Hernia Awareness," making it free again for people to use in support and research.

One year ago, I had never heard of CDH and was eleven weeks pregnant. Statistics say Ava already had a diaphragm that was not completely formed. Organs that should have been in her abdominal cavity floated freely into her chest cavity, taking up valuable lung space.

Fifty percent of babies born with CDH do not survive.

It occurs in about 1 in every 2,500 babies.

The cause of CDH is not known.

CDH occurs as often as spina bifida and cystic fibrosis, yet there is so little awareness. CDH strikes a baby every ten minutes, adding up to over six hundred thousand babies since the year 2000. That is over a quarter million babies who have died from this birth condition, but there is little research being done.

Below is a link to the CDH Research Bill. On the home page, you will find three easy steps to follow that allow you to send a letter to your senator or congressman asking for his or her support in passing the CDH Research Bill. I would be honored if you would spend a few minutes to send a letter "In Memory of Ava." I appreciate your support!

http://www.cdhbills.org/

Sweet Ava will be six months old this Good Friday. May you all have a wonderful Easter weekend.

With Love,
Jennifer

—∞—

CHAPTER 45

Mother's Day

When my sister, Kristi, and I were growing up, she would tease me to no end, and I'm sure I annoyed her daily. Sometimes she would catch my forearm with both her hands and twist them in opposite directions. It would cause an immediate sharp pain and then leave a burning sensation. I would run away, yelling "Mooooooom."

For the past few weeks, my heart has felt the same sharp pains followed by a lingering burn. I feel like there are hands on my heart, twisting in opposite directions and wringing out tears that gather in my eyes and sometimes stream down my face. *Thank God I can still reach out to my mom.* Maybe it's the recent replaying of 9/11 and the wounds that must open up again for the people directly affected by that tragedy. Obama's heartfelt words, "And yet we know that the worst images are those that were unseen to the world. The empty seat at the dinner table. Children who were forced to grow up without their mother or their father. Parents who would never know the feeling of their child's embrace. Nearly three thousand citizens taken from us, leaving a gaping hole in our hearts." Maybe it's the recent story I learned of our neighbors being blessed with a baby boy, Nathan, in an unexpected adoption. This precious baby, just a few months old, had been in three homes before finding this loving couple, who had been on an international adoption list for years. They started their regular daily routine one Monday and, by Wednesday, brought Nathan home. I remember his new mom telling us the story of shopping for a crib: "We'll take whatever you have in stock." *How ironic that our home was so prepared for a baby to come home . . . all the way down to the wipes*

114

being warm. I thought of giving them stacks of diapers and wipes, but that would require opening Ava's closet door. I love to sit in her nursery, look at her pictures, read and reflect. I'm not sure if my heart can handle looking at the clothes that she'll never wear. Maybe it's learning of a childhood friend's father who just passed away. *Why, why, why do we have to endure so much sadness?*

These few weeks between Easter and Mother's Day have been challenging. I continue to have happy moments that help ease the pain. Todd sends me flowers on the twenty-third of every month to celebrate our marriage. In April they came on the twenty-second, the day Ava turned six months. I had beautiful flowers to look at and remind me of how much I am loved. An employee returning from maternity leave showed up in my office with her new baby. He was born just a few weeks after Ava. I was overwhelmed and called Nancy: "Can you please ask her to leave. I can't handle seeing how big Ava would be." I ran into my bathroom and wept. Nancy appeared a few minutes later with a warm hug. She gave me a charm for my bracelet of a mother embracing a child. "Here, Jen, I got this for you for Mother's Day, but I want you to have it today." *What a true, dear friend to think of me months before Mother's Day.* We were walking home one evening after playing with the neighborhood kids. Another dad walked toward us, holding his new baby girl, and that sudden sting gripped my heart. *I bet London and Ava would have been the best of friends. Don't cry now, keep smiling and walking.* Then Jason says, "Momma Nenny, let's water the flowers when we get home. And I want to water Ava's, okay?" Mandy and Ally wrote a song for Ava. Some of their words: "Ava Elaine, you are so sweet. You touch my heart with your gentle hands. Every time I look at the sky . . . I think of you flying high and breathing easy." Yesterday I received an arrangement of beautiful red roses surrounding one pink rose with the note "An angel is thinking of you, from your aunts and uncles and with love from Ava."

Mother's Day is bittersweet for me. I have been anxious about it all week. I have the most wonderful, loving mother anyone could ever ask for. My life is filled with so many blessings. Today I thank God for my mom and all the wonderful mothers I know. I pray for peace and comfort to the moms who also have their sweet child in heaven. I pray for my friends and family that cannot see their moms to hug them today, because they are in heaven or too many miles away. *May the sweet memories of your mom make you smile today.*

Thank you for reading and allowing me to put my feelings into words. Sometimes that just makes me feel better. Happy Mother's Day!

CHAPTER 46

◆◆◆

One Year Ago

I read through some of Ava's journal last night, which began on September 30, 2010. Some things are clearer today than one year ago, when Ava's CDH journey started. As I read through some of Ava's critical hours, I remembered things that had run through my head but I left out because I was too scared to talk or write about them. I was determined to stay positive and never lost hope.

During a nightly round, a doctor was observing Ava's saturation levels. They were dropping because of a blood clot in her abdomen. I asked the doctor, "What can you do? Her foot is pale and cold. *Please do something!*" He replied, "We are doing all we can, and because she is on ECMO, there are more severe risks that we have to take into consideration. Losing her foot or leg is the lesser of two evils right now." *How would Ava be able to dance with only one foot? Ballet shoes come in a pair, not one.* I had never felt so helpless. A miracle happened that night; Ava was clot-free by the early morning sonogram. Through this past year, I have found peace, knowing she's dancing in heaven.

My because-of-Ava list has grown substantially this past year. I have so many blessings in my life because of her. Many of you generously donated to Ava's memorial fund, which was established at First Presbyterian Church, where Ava was enrolled and Jason goes to school. Todd and I wanted to donate something to the day school in Ava's memory. They needed and got a new buggy that holds six kiddos and is used every day at school. Mandy, Ally, and I went to Jason's class during art time, and we all made pictures for the buggy.

Mom and I spent a few days decorating it with pictures, and we put a plaque on the front and called it *The Ava Express*.

The church graciously allowed a baptismal font surrounded by a prayer labyrinth garden to be established in honor of Ava's life. The remainder of Ava's memorial fund will be used for this beautiful seventeenth-century baptismal font and plaque. The garden will be a place for us to reflect, give thanks and prayer, and cherish the precious memories held close in our hearts.

My motherly instinct has me planning for Ava's first birthday. The garden is almost complete and will be a perfect place for a celebration of Ava's life. I am sending invitations but do not want anyone to feel obligated to attend. My hope is that on this special day you are able to take a few minutes away from crazy, busy schedules and cherish what's most important in life.

For me, it's family, friends, and faith.

CHAPTER 47

Your First Birthday

Dear Sweet Ava,

At 11:32 p.m., daddy held me in his arms as we watched your birthday candle glow. It was a peaceful ending to a beautiful day. Our family and friends gathered at church for a celebration of life and a dedication service in your honor, Ava. First Presbyterian Church graciously dedicated a seventeenth-century baptismal font surrounded by a prayer labyrinth garden. It's a beautiful area that invites meditation and prayer, and it's a place we can remember the sweet memories of you that are held close in our hearts. As you enter the labyrinth, there's a plaque that reads,

In thanksgiving for the life of
Ava Elaine Dickerson
October 22, 2010–December 7, 2010
"She was a vehicle for a greater force"

Reverend Joe Clifford lead us in prayer and Scripture reading, and we sang "Jesus Loves Me" just like Grandma used to sing by your bed. "So teach us to count our days, that we might gain a wise heart" (Psalm 90:12 New International Version). Aunt Lori wrote a poem called "Happy Birthday, Ava." As she read the words, a mixture of happy and sad tears streamed down my face. My favorite verse: "Happy Birthday, Ava, for the lesson we've learned will not be in vain. You taught us how to never give up, and we won't ever be the same."

Ally and Mandy read the words of the song they wrote for you. I have faith that you watch over them every day and carry their tender hearts on your angel wings.

I shared a few stories and things that are on my because-of-Ava list. Family, friends, and my personal experiences have all contributed to this list, and it inspires me to be a better person. It's ongoing, and I think it will be that way forever as you continue to touch lives in your sweet, special way.

My girlfriend Carrie wrote the following:

> I just read your journal update from today. I loved hearing your beautiful letter to Ava again! I have to say that your posting came just when I needed it! I have been extremely stressed at work and frustrated with my company. I just found out that they put someone in a position that I had been interested in last year, but they never had the funding to open the position, until now I guess. Just as I was stewing over the news, your e-mail came over. It helped me to remember what is most important—my family! My work is a job that pays the bills and allows me to do things for my family. They are the most important thing in the world to me, and I need to continue to focus on that! I am lucky to have such a loving family that appreciates everything I do. So thank you for reminding me about what really matters.

Another CDH mom, Suzanne, read your obituary in the newspaper and reached out to me offering support. Suzanne's baby, Molly, lived only nineteen minutes after being born with a CDH. I sent Suzanne CDH awareness gear for Molly's seventh birthday this past spring. She had no idea there was an organization for CDH support, research, and awareness. Now she does, because of you, Ava.

Our friend Vince wrote the following to me one morning:

> As Tara and I prayed this morning over Ava, I came to the sad realization of how selfish our world is. Although we are blessed every day with God's gifts, such as the actual opportunity to wake up and see the light of day, we still go

on as if we deserve this life, never giving a second thought to those who are fighting for "this life." I know so many people who just don't get it and forget just how precious this life is. This sometimes includes myself. I welled up at the thought of an eight-day-old infant, fighting for what we take for granted. I also dedicated today to the thought of your daughter. Today Ava's strength has given me hope, and caused me to ask for forgiveness. Today I will stay strong and live in appreciation of all that I have, and I will do this because Ava wants me to.

A message from Todd's high school friend Bridget:

Dear Todd,

> After I saw your post yesterday, I read Jennifer's journal on CaringBridge. In the mere two hours or so it took me to read, I became attached to Ava. I have thought of nothing but you, Jennifer, Jason, and Jennifer's parents since then. I have said and will continue to say prayers for all of you. I have been reminded once again of how selfish I can be and to count my blessings. I am an ultrasound tech at two OB/GYN offices. I routinely check for diaphragmatic hernias when I do my scans and, because of Ava, will now check with even more scrutiny.

A sweet girl named Kelsey came up to me at your visitation service. She introduced herself to me as a friend of my cousin Kim. Kim was one of your biggest prayer warriors and shared your story with everyone. Kelsey followed your journey, and it inspired her to get a tattoo on her ankle that reads 47 Days. She told me that night that you have changed her life and makes her appreciate every single day she has.

Kelsey wrote an e-mail to me shortly after New Year's:

> My tattoo is all healed up, and I love sharing Ava's story with everyone who sees it. I still could not tell you why she has made such an impact on my life, but I'm thankful

she did. I find myself complaining less, praying more, and reflecting on what I want to do with my life. Finally, I have something personal to share, but after reading your entry from Friday, I almost feel guilty telling you. However, just like I felt I needed to get the tattoo, I feel like I need to say this. The same day I got your package, I found out I'm pregnant. Just seeing your name on the box made me cry. All my excitement and joy went away for a moment and all I could think of was why do I get to start a family and you had to lose your precious baby. It isn't fair! Thomas, my fiancé, looked at me and said, "Remember what you told me her memorial video said about she's a seed planted in all of us now to be better people, spouses, parents. She's going to be an inspiration to you forever, and an inspiration to our kids. You'll tell her story, and our kids will be thankful they're here and have parents who love them." Kelsey and Thomas decided they wanted to start a family of their own, because of Ava. So please let me introduce Kelsey and her daughter, Olivia Michele, born September 23.

One of the most life-changing things on my list is my faith in God. I accepted Jesus Christ as my Lord and Savior in high school but had always kept my faith to myself. I would occasionally thank God for blessings and ask for his help and guidance when I needed it. I would pray for family and friends in need but at my convenience. I believe God sent me a direct message through your journey that I needed to have a stronger faith. I witnessed miracles beginning with your birth and continuing with you overcoming obstacles that made the doctors scratch their heads. This past year, I have turned my broken heart to God, and He continues to heal. Through prayer and God's grace, I have a better understanding of why. I have found a church home here at First Presbyterian, and it's because of you, Ava.

Nancy at work told me that her son, Ethan, loves to have stories read to him. At bedtime when he asks, "Please Mommy, one more story," she reads it to him, because of you, Ava.

Many of our friends have told us they give extra hugs and kisses to their children because of you. They do not take any day for granted because of you, Ava.

I am more patient because of you, Ava.

Because of you we know some pretty amazing people we call Team Ava. They are our extended family at Children's and hold a very special place in our hearts. We have a surgeon on speed dial. That could come in handy with an almost-four-year-old who wants to go just as fast on his bike as the older kids in the neighborhood.

Speaking of Dr. Chen (we now call her by first name, Li Ern), we are establishing a charitable foundation for her do-good projects. Maybe we should call it "The Because of Ava Foundation." Li Ern is the kind of person who makes the world a better place. My dad describes her like you just want to wrap her up and take her with you everywhere you go. She once told me she does what she does because of the families she meets. And she does so much more than just performing surgery—some life saving, I'm sure—on children. Li Ern works just as much outside the operating room as she does inside, researching, speaking, teaching, and learning how to make the medical world better. The 2012 donation to your foundation will be made from the purchase of her photographs put on canvas for holiday gifts for my company's customers. She's a photographer by hobby, and her pictures look like paintings that belong in a museum. We have three in our home.

Your grandma and Aunt Lori kept in touch through daily text messages. They now know how to text-message with the best of them because of you, Ava.

I have made a commitment with a publishing company to make your journal into a book. My hope is to spread CDH awareness and give hope to people with broken hearts. You taught me more about love, faith, hope, and courage, without ever speaking a word. I feel your story can do the same. I will be a published author because of you, Ava.

Our close-knit family became even closer because of you. To your daddy, thank you for being strong and filling my empty arms. I know his heart hurts, too, and I pray that God continues to heal us.

During my pregnancy with you your daddy and I talked about how our family would be complete after your birth. You and Jason would be in the same school most of your years growing up, and he was so excited about being a big brother. When I was shopping for baby gear, a girlfriend told me, "Go with non-gender colors, just in case you want another!" I thought, *I love being pregnant, but this is it for me!* So we bought everything in pink. Having another baby will not replace you. You will always be our first daughter. But our next baby will have a guardian angel. I thank God every day for blessing us with another baby. I pray this baby is born healthy—ten fingers and ten toes and a fully developed diaphragm.

I thank God everyday for my family and friends, and that is definitely because of you, Ava. We concluded your celebration by releasing forty-seven butterflies, one for each day of your precious life here on earth. They symbolized the forty-seven days we journeyed with you, our angel. As they fluttered away, I admired them for taking off on their own journey of no less than a thousand miles, only on a wing and prayer. But they will make it, sweet Ava.

And so will we.

As I sit here, trying to find the words, I realize there is nothing I could say that all these wonderful people have not already said. As the grandfather of Ava, I feel very blessed in knowing that Ava's life touched so many people. As for me, *now I know what an angel looks like.*—Jack Rohde

A 17th Century Baptismal Font imported from England sits in the middle of a prayer labyrinth that invites prayer and meditation.

Ava's dedication plaque sits in from of the baptismal font and is adorned with a quote from Dr. Thomas, "She was a vehicle for a greater force"

Ava's 1ˢᵗ Birthday

In prayer with Reverend Joseph Clifford

Taking Flight

The Labyrinth Garden

CPSIA information can be obtained
at www.ICGtesting.com
Printed in the USA
LVHW090207100820
662786LV00008B/23/J